INSTANT BIBLE STUDIES

JIM BURNS AND MIKE DeVRIES

Gospel Light

Gospel Light is an evangelical Christian publisher dedicated to serving the local church. We believe God's vision for Gospel Light is to provide church leaders with biblical, user-friendly materials that will help them evangelize, disciple and minister to children, youth and families.

It is our prayer that this Gospel Light resource will help you discover biblical truth for your own life and help you minister to youth. May God richly bless you.

For a free catalog of resources from Gospel Light, please contact your Christian supplier or contact us at 1-800-4-GOSPEL or www.gospellight.com.

PUBLISHING STAFF
William T. Greig, Chairman
Kyle Duncan, Publisher
Dr. Elmer L. Towns, Senior Consulting Publisher
Pam Weston, Senior Editor
Patti Pennington Virtue, Associate Editor
Jeff Kempton, Editorial Assistant
Hilary Young, Editorial Assistant
Bayard Taylor, M.Div., Senior Editor, Biblical and Theological Issues
Kevin Parks, Cover Designer
Roseanne Richardson, Cover Production
Debi Thayer, Designer

ISBN 0-8307-2919-4
© 2002 Gospel Light, Ventura, CA 93006
All rights reserved.
Printed in the U.S.A.

How to Make Clean Copies from This Book

You may make copies of portions of this book with a clean conscience if:
- you (or someone in your organization) are the original purchaser;
- you are using the copies you make for a noncommercial purpose (such as teaching or promoting your ministry) within your church or organization;
- you follow the instructions provided in this book.

However, it is ILLEGAL for you to make copies if:
- you are using the material to promote, advertise or sell a product or service other than for ministry fund-raising;
- you are using the material in or on a product for sale;
- you or your organization are **not** the original purchaser of this book.

By following these guidelines you help us keep our products affordable.
Thank you,
Gospel Light

Permission to make photocopies or to reproduce by any other mechanical or electronic means in whole or in part of any designated* page, illustration or activity in this book is granted only to the original purchaser and is intended for noncommercial use within a church or other Christian organization. None of the material in this book may be reproduced for any commercial promotion, advertising or sale of a product or service. Sharing of the material in this book with other churches or organizations not owned or controlled by the original purchaser is also prohibited. All rights reserved.

*Pages with the following notation can be legally reproduced:
© 2002 Gospel Light. Permission to photocopy granted. *Instant Bible Studies*

CONTENTS

Small Group Bible Study Outlines—
A Study of James

Scripture Reference Index

MIKE'S DEDICATION

To Madison—Every time I look into your eyes, see your smile or see you crawling to find me, I am overwhelmed. You are a precious gift of God to our family. My prayer for you is that as you grow, you will always know that I will always love you.

—Daddy

SPECIAL THANKS

To all the students at churches, camps and conferences who have joined me in opening the Word of God and have been changed by what we encountered there.

To Dawnielle Hodgman—There is no way this project would have happened without you. Thanks for your hard work and long hours. Working alongside you is one of life's great joys! Thanks, my friend!

To Jamie, Joshua, Megan, Mikayla and Madison—Thank you not only for loaning Daddy to compile this book but also for allowing me to open our lives and share so many stories with others. You are the joy of my life and I love you!

To John Werhas, Jon Irving and Dave Rembert—Thanks for teaching me what it means to love the Word.

To my God—Opening Your Word and communicating Your truth is my greatest desire; it is like breath unto my soul. May all I say and do be done for Your glory!

Open my eyes that I may see wonderful things in your law (Psalm 119:18).

—Mike

INTRODUCTION

Have you ever heard a great sermon and thought to yourself, *This outline or Scripture will absolutely work for my next talk as well*? Of course you have. I am proud to say that almost every great speaker in America has at one time or another given me a message to pass on to the students and families I speak with. When you find that right outline or message, it is a gift because, as you well know, it is not always easy coming up with new material week after week, month after month.

This book is filled with some of our best Bible study messages and small group outlines. They have worked with kids. Obviously, no message is so complete that you won't have to adapt it to your personal experience, but we have tried to bring most of the important ingredients of Bible messages and small group material to you so that you can quickly adapt these messages to become your own.

Much of this material is the work of Mike DeVries. Mike is one of the most creative, articulate and innovative youth communicators in the world today. He knows how to reach inside a student's heart for a positive God-honoring response. I always appreciate his commitment to using a scriptural text to lead students directly to God's Word on each subject.

In a small way we have opened up our files and hearts to you. We love to craft practical, helpful messages and small group experiences from a biblical perspective. What you have in this book is our best shot to serve you with our finest material. We hope it helps. We are so grateful for your willingness to make an eternal difference in the lives of young people and their families.

Blessings,
Jim Burns, Ph.D.
President, YouthBuilders

BIBLE STUDY MESSAGE OUTLINES

Overview

ATTITUDE OR ATTIRUDE? THE CHOICE IS UP TO YOU!

TOPIC
Our attitude toward our families

DESCRIPTION
For better or worse, our families impact us. While we may never be able to change our family circumstances, we can control our attitude toward our families and have a positive influence on them. This message examines the attitude Jesus demonstrated and applies His attitude model directly to our family relationships.

KEY VERSE
"Your attitude should be the same as that of Christ Jesus." Philippians 2:5

BIBLICAL BASIS
Philippians 2:5-7; 3:12; Colossians 2:13-14; 3:13; 1 Thessalonians 5:18

THE BIG IDEA
Our family circumstances may never change, but our attitude can—and that makes all the difference.

PREPARATION
*   The video *Mrs. Doubtfire* (20th Century Fox, 1993)
*   A TV and a VCR

Cue the video to the beginning of the movie where the parents (played by Sally Field and Robin Williams) are having an argument and resolve that the best thing to do is to get a divorce. You'll end the clip at the scene showing the children secretly listening on the staircase.

Outline

ATTITUDE OR ATTIRUDE?
THE CHOICE IS UP TO YOU!

> **The Big Idea**
> Our family circumstances may never change, but our attitude can—and that makes all the difference.

INTRODUCTION

Show the clip from *Mrs. Doubtfire*; then transition by explaining: **Our families can have an incredible impact on who we are as people, what we value and how we see life and family. Yet we can also have an impact on our families if we choose to. Each of us can impact our families, not by changing the people around us, but by changing ourselves! We can't change others, only God can.**

> **Reminder:** It is illegal to *rent* a video at the video store and show it to your group without first having purchased a license to do so. A blanket movie license can be bought by your church that will allow you to show virtually any movie to your group or congregation for one year by calling the Motion Picture Licensing Corporation at 1-800-462-8855.

So if we want to change or impact our families, we need to let God change or impact our attitude. Our attitude is a choice. We choose how to respond to situations, or circumstances. Read Philippians 2:5-7 and continue: **In order to impact our families, we need to have the attitude that Jesus had.**

BODY OF THE MESSAGE

There are four choices that we need to make in order to impact our families by having an attitude like Jesus.

I. Have an Attitude of Forgiveness—Colossians 3:13

    A. No one is perfect.

    B. No matter how badly we've been hurt by others, we need to choose to forgive.

        We should forgive because God has forgiven us.

    C. We need to choose not to harbor bitterness.
        1. True forgiveness brings freedom from bitterness.
        2. True forgiveness brings healing to relationships.
    D. True forgiveness means making choices.
        1. Live with the consequences.
        2. Leave the past behind.
        3. Let those you forgive off your hook (but that doesn't mean they're off *God's* hook!).
    E. Are we choosing to forgive? It will impact our families!

II. Have an Attitude of Unconditional Love—Colossians 2:13-14

    A. God has an incredible, unconditional love for us. He loves us for who we are, not because of anything that we do.
    B. Read Colossians 2:14. We are given a glimpse of God's unconditional love for us.
    C. Unconditional love has no strings attached; it's not "I'll love you if," "I'll love you when" or "I'll love you only."
        1. Do we love our families with that type of love? Or is our love conditional?
        2. God offers us an "I'll love you regardless" love and desires that we offer that same love to our families.

III. Have an Attitude of Servanthood—Philippians 2:5-7

    A. One of the biggest ways we can impact our families is by having an attitude of servanthood (and it can be a difficult attitude to maintain).
    B. Read Philippians 2:7. Jesus is our model for servanthood.
    C. Being a servant means we must do several things.
        1. Give up our rights sometimes.
        2. Seek humility.
        3. Ask ourselves, *What can I do to serve or help?*
    D. Are we seeking to serve our families? That attitude will make all the difference.

IV. Have an Attitude of Gratitude—1 Thessalonians 5:18

    A. An attitude of gratitude means having a "No matter what happens" attitude.
    B. Read Thessalonians 5:18. If there's one choice that can change our entire attitude, it's being thankful.
        1. We are not asked to be thankful *for* every circumstance but to be thank-

ful *in* every circumstance.

2. We will see our attitudes change when we try to look at our circumstances from God's perspective—look for what good can come out of it.

C. Knowing that we go through everything for a reason, we can thank God for the family He has given each of us, regardless of our family situation. Can we honestly say that we are thankful for our families? If not, we need to look at our attitudes.

CHALLENGE/ACTION STEPS

1. Progression is the key to change. We are all in the process of growing and progressing.

2. Read Philippians 3:12 and then take some time to pray before choosing one of the following four attitudes to work on:

- Who do you need to forgive? (See Colossians 3:13.)
- Is your love unconditional or do you place conditions on people to earn or keep your love? (See Colossians 2:13-14.)
- Do you have a servant's heart for your family? (See Philippians 2:5-7.)
- Do you have an attitude of gratitude, thanking God even during difficult circumstances? (See 1 Thessalonians 5:18.)

ATTITUDE OR ATTIRUDE?
THE CHOICE IS UP TO YOU!

1. How do you react to the following statement? "Our family circumstances may never change, but our attitude can—and that makes all the difference."

2. If you could describe your family in one word, what would it be?

3. If you could change one thing about your family, what would it be?

4. Which of the four attitudes is the toughest for you personally? Why?

5. What is one action step you can take this week to change that attitude?

Overview

Living Life at 120 MPH

TOPIC
Balance and priorities

DESCRIPTION
We live life at a breathless pace. Days and weeks pass us by before we even realize it. If we are not proactive in guarding what is important in our lives, we are in real danger of losing our focus. This message examines three essential questions every student must ask him- or herself in order to keep first things first.

KEY VERSE
"So the Twelve gathered all the disciples together and said, 'It would not be right for us to neglect the ministry of the word of God in order to wait on tables. Brothers, choose seven men from among you who are known to be full of the Spirit and wisdom. We will turn this responsibility over to them and will give our attention to prayer and the ministry of the word.'" Acts 6:2-4

BIBLICAL BASIS
Acts 6:1-7

THE BIG IDEA
What is good is often the enemy of what is *best*.

PREPARATION
- A video showing the Indianapolis 500 or some other racing event. If possible, the video should show a high-speed crash.
- A TV and a VCR

Cue the video to a minute or so before a significant high-speed crash.

Outline

LIVING LIFE AT 120 MPH

> **The Big Idea**
> What is good is often the enemy of what is *best*.

INTRODUCTION

Play the video clip, ending it just after the crash scene; then transition by explaining: **Sometimes we rush through life convinced that more is better. The busier we are, the more effective—or the more important—we think we are.**

> **Consider This**
> Acts 6:1-7 is a descriptive view of a very busy people.
> 1. The church was growing dramatically. With that growth came tremendous need.
> 2. The Twelve were busy about the work of God, but their busyness had its price—it kept them from spending time with God.

We can become so preoccupied with doing even good things that we neglect the most important thing of all—our relationship with God.

BODY OF THE MESSAGE

If you're feeling so busy in your life that you are missing out on life itself, there are three questions you need to ask yourself.

I. Who Is the Most Important?—Acts 6:4

A. We can be so busy about the business of God that we miss being with God.

B. It's important that we don't become so busy serving God that we miss knowing Him.

C. The most important thing you can do to maintain balance in your life is take care of your relationship with God.

D. You can't live—or give—from an empty well.

II. What Is the Most Important?—Acts 6:2

A. Each of us needs to take an honest look at the busyness of our lives and ask ourselves three questions.
1. *Is this good or is it the best?*
2. *Of all the things that I'm involved in, what is really necessary?*
3. *What is really important for me to be involved in?*

B. We can be involved in so many good things, that we can crowd out the best things such as building relationships with God and others.

C. We live our lives a mile wide and an inch deep—and wonder why we feel so stretched in life.

D. It's an ongoing battle to fight against being too busy to spend time with God, but it's a battle we must face—and win.

III. What Is the Most Effective?—Acts 6:3

A. Being effective means operating within your calling and giftedness. The Twelve knew what they did best and decided to give to other people the things that they did not do as well.

B. We should take a good look at our lives and the things we feel called and gifted to do.
1. What are the things that we are best at doing and not just good at doing?
2. How much time do we spend developing and exercising that which we are best at?

C. If we don't make some proactive decisions regarding our time, someone else will. If the devil can't make you bad, he'll make you busy.

CHALLENGE/ACTION STEPS

1. Stop—Take some time alone this week.
2. Look—Examine your life (activities, values and time).
3. Listen—Seek God's perspective on *who* is most important and *what* is most important and most effective in your life.

LIVING LIFE AT 120 MPH

1. What are some things you need to keep in balance in your life?

2. What makes it tough to find balance in your life? What are some of the barriers you face?

3. What *should* the top five priorities in your life be? List them.

4. Take a look at your list of priorities and think about how you live your life—how and where you spend your time. Are those really the top five priorities in your life?

5. What are three changes you can make this week to redirect your priorities where they should be?

Overview

HOW TO LIVE UNNATURALLY—SUPERNATURALLY

TOPIC
Living as a Christian in a non-Christian world

DESCRIPTION
Being a follower of Jesus is a call to live life differently. Our lives should be the mark that sets us apart from those around us. Others should see a transformation in our lives that can come only from God. Sadly, too often our lives don't reflect this dramatic change. This message focuses on the transformation of life that Christ calls us to and reminds us that the only way we can live differently is through the power of Christ.

KEY VERSE
"Live in harmony with one another. Do not be proud, but be willing to associate with people of low position. Do not be conceited. Do not repay anyone evil for evil. Be careful to do what is right in the eyes of everybody." Romans 12:16-17

BIBLICAL BASIS
Romans 12:1-3,16-21; 1 Peter 1:15-16

THE BIG IDEA
As Christians, we are called to live our lives differently.

PREPARATION
• A three- to five-minute video of a cartoon superhero (e.g., Superman or Spiderman) displaying superhuman power
• A TV and a VCR

Outline

HOW TO LIVE UNNATURALLY—SUPERNATURALLY

The Big Idea
As Christians, we are called to live our lives differently.

INTRODUCTION

Show the video clip as a visual introduction to the topic of living supernaturally. Ask: **If you could have any superpower, what would it be and why?** Allow a few responses; then explain: **God calls us to live our lives differently from the rest of the world** (see 1 Peter 1:15-16)—**to live supernaturally. His call requires us to use some serious superpowers that only He can provide.**

There are three ingredients for living differently.

BODY OF THE MESSAGE

Living as a Christian in a non-Christian world means living differently from others around us. In a world where so many are focused on their own desires, Christians are called upon to live unselfishly in humility, honor and peace.

I. Live in Humility, Not Pride—Romans 12:16

  A. Live your life humbly, without pride or conceit.
    1. Living a prideful life is easy. Pride focuses on self. It says "Look at me!"
    2. Living humbly is unnatural. Humility focuses on God and others.
  B. God calls us to live differently.
    1. Read Romans 12:3. Don't act like you're too important, but have an accurate view of who you are.
    2. Hang out with all types of people.
    3. Don't be a know-it-all—be teachable!
  C. When we choose to live humbly, our lives will be different.

II. Live in Honor, Not Dishonor—Romans 12:17

  A. Do everything with honor.
    1. Living with honor is unnatural—we'd rather get revenge.

2. Read Romans 12:17. When we repay evil for evil, we do not live honorably.

B. God commands our lives to be marked by honor.

1. We are to be consistent in all that we do.

2. We are to be trustworthy in all that we say.

III. Live in Harmony, Not Hostility—Romans 12:18-21

A. Read Romans 12:18. God reminds us to live in peace with those around us.

B. We are going to encounter people in our lives who will hurt us by what they say or do.

C. When we are hurt, our natural response is to seek revenge, to let those who hurt us know how it feels.

1. Seeking revenge isn't the answer.

2. Revenge can lead to a cycle of vengeful acts by those who are hurt.

D. God says, "Live differently!"

1. Seek to live in peace with others, working through tough situations.

2. God is a better judge than you are. Give up your right to seek revenge; leave the situation in God's hands, placing your trust in His justice.

3. Seek to do good to those who do wrong to you.

CHALLENGE/ACTION STEPS

1. Be honest.
   - Is your life self-centered or God-centered?
   - If you call yourself a Christian, is your life really different?
   - How are you doing in living in humility, honor and harmony?

2. Be active.
   - Is there anything you need to confess, or admit, to God?
   - Is there someone you need to ask forgiveness from?
   - Is there an attitude you need to change?
   - Is there a relationship you need to mend?

3. Be in touch.
   - Read Romans 12:1-2. Let God transform you! He will change you and supply all the power you need to live life differently.
   - The only way we can live life supernaturally is to remain close to Jesus.

HOW TO LIVE UNNATURALLY—SUPERNATURALLY

1. If you could have any superhuman power, what would you want and why?

2. What is one thing you have tried lately that you were totally unqualified to do, ill-equipped for or lacked any knowledge of what to do? What was the result?

3. What makes the Christian life impossible to live without the empowering of God?

4. Which area in your walk with God seems to be the most difficult right now?

5. How can you rely on God to help you through that situation?

6. Spend time together in prayer for each person concerning questions 4 and 5.

Overview

LIVE THE LIFE

TOPIC
Living life focused on Christ

DESCRIPTION
Our world today tries to sell us on what life should be all about, but what the world tries to sell us is no life at all. Real life is found in Jesus Christ. John 10:10 reminds us that Jesus came to give us life and life to the full. Rather than settle for a cheap imitation of the real thing, this message guides students to where real life is found—in the person of Jesus Christ.

KEY VERSE
"Since, then, you have been raised with Christ, set your hearts on things above, where Christ is seated at the right hand of God. Set your minds on things above, not on earthly things. For you died, and your life is now hidden with Christ in God. When Christ, who is your life, appears, then you also will appear with him in glory." Colossians 3:1-4

BIBLICAL BASIS
Isaiah 33:6; Matthew 6:19-21,24; Mark 8:34-38; John 10:10; 14:6; Colossians 3:1-4,7-10,12-16; Hebrews 12:1-2

THE BIG IDEA
Living life as a Christian is living the real life.

PREPARATION
- Two gift boxes, similar in size
- A $5 bill
- Nice gift wrap and a bow
- Transparent tape
- The funnies section of a Sunday paper
- Stapler

Place the $5 bill in one of the boxes and fill the other box with trash (be sure you know which box is which). Carefully wrap the trash box with the paper and ribbon; then haphazardly wrap the money box with the newspaper, using the stapler instead of tape. After you've wrapped the money box, toss it around a little to dent it and make it look less than inviting.

Outline

LIVE THE LIFE

> **The Big Idea**
> Living life as a Christian is living the real life.

INTRODUCTION

> **Object Lesson**
> Ask two volunteers to step forward and pick a box to open. Let them know that they can keep whatever is in the box they pick.

Introduce the message with the object lesson; then explain: **You can't judge what's inside (the value) by the outside (the hype). Too many people live their lives enamored by the hype, buying into what they think something is only to find out it wasn't what it seemed.**

Real life has meaning and significance, and that's what Jesus wants to give each of us (see John 10:10). It's the greatest adventure you could ever know.

BODY OF THE MESSAGE

There are three targets to aim toward to experience the thrill of real life.

I. Set Your Heart—Colossians 3:1

A. "For where your treasure is, there your heart will be also" (Matthew 6:21).
   1. What is it that we value in life? What do we treasure?
   2. The things we treasure have special value and meaning in our lives.
   3. We make time for treasured things.
B. The things that we treasure are the things that we set our hearts on.
   1. We can set our hearts on empty promises and end up brokenhearted.
   2. We can set our hearts on real life—Jesus Christ—and be filled with His love.

C. God calls us to set our hearts "on things above" (Colossians 3:1). We are to focus on the promise of our eternity in heaven, rather than the temporary things on Earth.
   1. Read Matthew 6:19-20. Earthly things are temporary, but heaven is forever.
   2. Read Isaiah 33:6. God is the foundation we can count on. He is the key to real treasure and real life.

II. Set Your Mind—Colossians 3:2

A. "You cannot serve both God and Money" (Matthew 6:24). What we value most will fill our minds.
B. What we spend time thinking and dreaming about will impact how we live our lives.
   1. What is it that we pursue in life?
   2. What is it that we spend time thinking or daydreaming about?
   3. What we pursue in life could be empty and hollow or filled with the real life offered by Christ.

III. Set Your Sights on the Goal—Colossians 3:12-16

A. Who are we living for?
   1. Read Colossians 3:7-10. Are we ready to give up our sinful earthly pleasures in exchange for the life Christ offers?
   2. Read Colossians 3:12. Are we clothed in "compassion, kindness, humility, gentleness and patience" or do we live our lives in selfishness? When we live life for ourselves, we find out that it's lonely, lacking real life. We settle for a cheap imitation of the real thing.
B. Read Colossians 3:3-4. Jesus is real life.
   1. Read John 14:6. Real life is found in Jesus alone.
      a. It's our choice to make: will we live for ourselves or by God's ideals?
      b. If you want to live a real life, then choose to live your life for the only One who is the real life—Jesus Christ.
   2. Read Mark 8:34-38. When we choose to follow Christ, our old lives change and new real life is begun.

CHALLENGE/ACTION STEPS
   1. The choice is yours: will you believe the hype or will you search for real life?
   2. Read Hebrews 12:1-2 and get R-E-A-L!

R—*Realize* that real life is only found in Jesus Christ.

E—*Eliminate* stuff that holds you back.

- If there's something that you know is holding you back, let it go.
- Maybe it's how you spend your time or what you allow yourself to dwell on.
- Maybe you know that you're living for yourself only.

A—*Allow* Jesus to be your main focus; focus your eyes on the goal.

L—*Look* and lean on Jesus. He is there to help you, to see you through.

LIVE THE LIFE

1. What are the things that the world seeks after?

2. What are the things that God desires we seek after?

3. What is the difference between the two?

4. What are the things that you treasure in life? What are you pursuing? Are they truly fulfilling?

5. What changes do you need to make to seek after the things of God?

Overview

ORIGINAL MASTERPIECE OR CHEAP IMITATION?

TOPIC
Living life as an original masterpiece of God

DESCRIPTION
God has created each and every one of us as a unique and original person. Our heavenly Father thought through every facet of our lives, yet many times we live our lives as replicas of everyone else or according to others' expectations. The goal of this message is to open the eyes of students to the influences and perspectives they hold about themselves and their value, and to encourage them to choose to live their lives as the original masterpieces that they are—handcrafted by God Himself.

KEY VERSE
"Therefore, I urge you, brothers, in view of God's mercy, to offer your bodies as living sacrifices, holy and pleasing to God—this is your spiritual act of worship. Do not conform any longer to the pattern of this world, but be transformed by the renewing of your mind. Then you will be able to test and approve what God's will is—his good, pleasing and perfect will.

"For by the grace given me I say to every one of you: Do not think of yourself more highly than you ought, but rather think of yourself with sober judgment, in accordance with the measure of faith God has given you." Romans 12:1-3

BIBLICAL BASIS
Psalm 139:13-18; Romans 6:12-14; 12:1-3

THE BIG IDEA
We should live our lives like the original masterpieces God created us to be.

PREPARATION
- Three containers of play dough

Outline

ORIGINAL MASTERPIECE OR CHEAP IMITATION?

> **The Big Idea**
> We should live our lives like the original masterpieces God created us to be.

INTRODUCTION

Read Psalm 139:13-18. Explain: **We can sometimes look at our lives and see no value at all, but God does because He created each and every person on Earth. God doesn't want us to be replicas of everyone else or to live as others expect us to. Each one of us is an original masterpiece, handcrafted by the Creator, with His fingerprints all over us. God's desire is that we live lives that are non-conforming—not trying to be like everyone else or like what we think we should be. God's desire is that we live lives that are transformed.**

Object Lesson Option 1

Begin by promoting your newfound talent as an artist. Explain that you have been studying art in your off time and have begun to experiment with a new form of artistic expression: spontaneous sculpting. Act excited as you continue to explain that you'd like to share what you've learned with the group, and ask students to call out ideas for an object to sculpt. Wait until someone suggests an object that is ridiculously difficult to make (a statue of Abraham Lincoln, a 1939 Roadster—you get the idea). Once you've decided on an object, bring out the clay (the play dough) and spend about 30 seconds sculpting—making sure to look seriously intent on the task at hand, of course. When you're finished, present your "masterpiece" to your audience and ask: **How does our object look—anything like the original?** Explain: **This might not look exactly like the item it was supposed to resemble, but it's definitely unique! There's not another one exactly like it on the face of the planet. Even real artists' sculptures don't always look the way you and I might expect them to be when we learn what they're supposed to resemble. Some of those sculptures are very valuable, even though they may not look like they should according to you or me. What's important is that they are valuable to their creators, just as we are valued by ours.**

Object Lesson Option 2
Ask a volunteer to come forward and create a sculpture. As explained in Option 1, ask for ideas from the audience for items to sculpt, selecting the most impossible to sculpt. Allow the volunteer 30 seconds to complete the sculpture; then apply the discussion outlined in Option 1.

BODY OF THE MESSAGE

There are four changes we need to make in order to live like the original creations God made.

I. Change Our Habits—Romans 12:1

    A. All of us have good and bad habits.
        1. We make New Year's resolutions to try to change our bad habits.
        2. Most resolutions fail because we can't change ourselves.
    B. Read Romans 6:12-14. Some of us are being controlled.
    C. When we become Christians, God frees us, but there's still a choice to be made. Choose to honor God by what you do. Think of what He's done for each of us.

II. Change Who Influences Us—Romans 12:2

    A. Often we live our lives like potter's clay, being molded by whatever pressure is exerted upon us. (Suggestion: Take a lump of play dough and squeeze it into different shapes as you continue to talk.)
        1. Are we going to live our lives for others or are we going to live our lives as new and different creations?
        2. *Who* really influences us (e.g., friends' expectations, celebrities' worldviews, God, etc.)?
        3. *What* really influences our values and what we desire to be and do (e.g., media messages, friends, parents, etc.)?
    B. God wants to transform and change us. He wants to create new passions, new influences, new values and new behaviors in our lives.

III. Change Our Direction—Romans 12:2

    A. It's very sad to think that we might gather together next year and sit in our same chairs completely unchanged from what we are now.
    B. God has so much planned for each of us. Read Romans 12:2. Do you want to know what God wants for you?
        1. God wants us to know His plans and desires for us. Are we ready to hear Him?

2. Are we willing to say "God, I'm willing to follow Your directions and desires"?

C. We don't know what's in store for us in the years to come, but we can choose to follow the One who knows everything!

IV. Change Our Perspective—Romans 12:3

A. Perspective is what we value and where our personal value comes from.
   1. Is our personal value based on something changeable or unchangeable?
   2. Do we gain our value from our looks? From our intelligence? From our abilities? From our choice of friends?
   3. Physical things are transitory; they come and go. What can our personal value be based upon that isn't transitory?

C. As Christians, we need to have a different perspective.
   1. As Christians, our value needs to come from something unchangeable: God.
   2. Our value is what *God* thinks of us, not what we or others think.

D. God's love is based, not on what we do, what we have or how we perform, but on who we *are*—original masterpieces created by a loving heavenly Father.

CHALLENGE/ACTION STEPS

Read Romans 12:1-3 and consider the following questions:
- God created you to be an original masterpiece—do you live like one?
- What are some habits that you need to deal with this week? (See verse 1.)
- Who and what are the influences in your life? (See verse 2.)
- Who do you seek for direction in life? (See verse 2.)
- Where do you find your value? (See verse 3.)

ORIGINAL MASTERPIECE OR CHEAP IMITATION?

1. What is one thing that spoke to you during this message?

2. What are some habits that you need to deal with this week?

3. What are some of the influences that mold your life? How do you see those influences impacting your life, your values and your decisions?

4. Who do you go to for direction in your life?

5. Why is it sometimes tough to seek God for direction in life?

6. What are the things you value in life? (Hint: The things we spend most of our time doing and being involved with are usually indicative of what we truly value.)

7. Where do you find most of your personal value in life?

8. What are three ways in which you can seek God's value for your life this week?

Overview

AND YOU CALL YOURSELF A CHRISTIAN!

TOPIC
Unity in the midst of differences, Christian freedom and responsibility

DESCRIPTION
Christians don't always agree; however, in spite of our differences we are called to be a unified people under the banner of Jesus Christ. This message examines Romans 14 and Paul's encouragement to be unified in the midst of Christian freedoms. His call is clear. We have freedom, but we also have responsibility.

KEY VERSE
"Therefore let us stop passing judgment on one another. Instead, make up your mind not to put any stumbling block or obstacle in your brother's way." Romans 14:13

BIBLICAL BASIS
Romans 12:3; 14:1-23

THE BIG IDEA
As Christians we are called to unity in spite of our differences.

PREPARATION
None

OUTLINE

AND YOU CALL YOURSELF A CHRISTIAN!

The Big Idea
As Christians we are called to unity in spite of our differences.

INTRODUCTION

Christians don't always agree. What is believed okay for some falls into a gray area for others.

Consider This
Wide disagreements exist today in our churches over certain practices. A Christian from the South was repelled by a swimming party for both men and women, and then he offended his Northern brother by lighting up a cigarette. At an international conclave for missionaries, a woman from Asia could not wear sandals with a clear conscience. A Christian from western Canada thought it worldly for a Christian acquaintance to wear a wedding ring, and a woman from Europe thought it almost immoral for a wife not to wear a ring that signaled her status. A man from Denmark was pained to even watch British Bible school students play football, while the British students shrank from his pipe smoking.[1]

But what about us? Do we have any differences between us and other believers? You bet!

Object Lesson
Have students stand. Designate one side of the room as the "agree" side, the other the "disagree" side. Read through the following statements and instruct students to vote whether they agree or disagree with each statement by moving to the side of the room that matches their answer. If time allows, consider asking a few students to share the reason for their answers—encourage them to back up their positions with Scripture.
- There are certain situations in which it is okay to lie.
- Social drinking is okay, as long as you are over the age of 21.
- Dancing doesn't really glorify God.
- Christians shouldn't listen to secular music.

What do we do to handle differences? We are called to aim for unity, not judgment of others.

BODY OF THE MESSAGE

Romans 14 shows us five foundations for unity.

I. Accept One Another—Romans 14:1-2

A. Read Romans 14:1. God calls us to genuinely accept one another. The term "weak" in this verse refers to being weak in conscience/assurance in faith to do something; indecisive.[2]

B. Read Romans 12:2-4. Don't look down on one another. No matter who we are or where we're from, we are called to accept one another.
  1. We are to accept others wholeheartedly, in spite of differences, with no hidden agenda or motive to change who they are.
  2. Read Romans 14:5-6. We are called to distinguish between the nonessentials and the essentials of faith.

C. Read Romans 14:7-12. We are all called to accept the lordship of Christ.
  1. As Christians, our allegiance is to Christ, not to nonessentials.
  2. There is room for everyone in the Body of Christ, no matter who they are.

D. Some things just don't matter; we need to learn what does.

II. Show Concern for One Another—Romans 14:13-15

A. We are reminded not to put a stumbling block or obstacle in the path of others.
  1. A stumbling block is something carelessly left.[3]
  2. An obstacle is something deliberately left.[4]

B. When we exercise our freedom in Christ, we are reminded not to cause another brother to stumble.

C. Read Romans 14:15. Paul speaks directly to any behavior that distresses another's conscience. The key is to act in love and to balance love and liberty.

D. We should not cause another Christian to go against his or her conscience by exercising our freedoms in Christ.

III. Serve One Another—Romans 14:16-18

A. Paul reminds us to live as citizens of the kingdom of God—as servants.

B. We are to live our lives not in legalism but in grace.

1. The kingdom of God is not about legalism (i.e., the Pharisees versus Jesus).

2. The Pharisees focused on the externals; Jesus focused on the internals.

C. According to Romans 14:17, the kingdom is about "righteousness, peace and joy in the Holy Spirit." Paul calls us to set aside those freedoms and serve one another.

IV. Build Up One Another—Romans 14:19-21

A. We must always ask ourselves, *Is what I'm doing building others up, even if I consider them to be weak Christians?*

1. If we cannot say yes, then we need to reconsider what we're doing.

2. When we ask this question and decide to refrain from our actions, we actually show love, putting others first before our liberty and ourselves.

B. We are called to seek those things that bring about mutual benefit, not just benefit for one person.

V. Give Grace to One Another—Romans 14:22-23

A. Read Romans 14:22. Paul gives advice to the strong.

B. What you believe about neutral things is between you and God. Keep it that way. You will be blessed if you don't hurt others by exercising your freedom before those weak in faith.

Consider This

Two of the most famous Christians in the Victorian era in England were Charles Spurgeon and Joseph Parker, both mighty preachers of the gospel. Early in their ministries they fellowshiped and even exchanged pulpits. Then they had a disagreement, and the reports got into the newspapers. Spurgeon accused Parker of being unspiritual because he attended the theater. Interestingly enough, Spurgeon smoked cigars, a practice many believers condemned. In fact, on one occasion someone asked Spurgeon about his cigars, and he said he did not smoke to excess. When asked what he meant by excess, he waggishly answered, "No more than two at a time." Spurgeon, at the height of his fame, was one day walking down the street and saw a sign which read "We sell the cigar that Charles Spurgeon smokes," whereupon Spurgeon gave up the habit. He came to see that what was for him a freedom might cause others to stumble.[5]

C. Read Romans 14:23. Paul's advice to the weak: If you are not fully convinced and sense doubt in your heart, it's better not to do it! Do everything with a clear conscience!

CHALLENGE/ACTION STEPS

Confused about what to do in a situation? Read Romans 14 and ask yourself:

- *Am I accepting or rejecting?* (See verses 1-12.)
- *Am I causing another to stumble?* (See verses 13-15.)
- *Am I being an accurate reflection of the Kingdom?* (See verses 16-18.)
- *Am I striving for mutual benefit or just my own?* (See verses 19-21.)
- *Am I doing this by faith, with a clear conscience?* (See verses 22-23.)

Notes

1. R. Kent Hughes, *Romans—Righteousness from Heaven* (Wheaton, IL: Crossway Books, 1991), p. 259.
2. Ibid.
3. Ibid., p. 268.
4. Ibid.
5. Ibid., pp. 263, 273.

AND YOU CALL YOURSELF A CHRISTIAN!

1. What are some of the gray issues in our world today?

2. What makes decisions on some of those gray issues so difficult?

3. Which of the foundations—basic to Christian beliefs—is the hardest for you? Why?

4. What are three action steps that you can take to work on that foundation?

Overview

THE CRY OF THE CROSS

TOPIC
The cross of Christ—a Good Friday message

DESCRIPTION
The Cross stands at the center of all of Christianity. Without the Cross, there is no hope. There is no hope for salvation. There is no hope of reconciliation. Christ went to the cross as the ultimate witness to the glory of God—that a holy God would have to go to such a price to redeem His glory, as well as us. The Cross came at a terrible cost, but more terrible yet is the call that comes with it, a call to surrender and die. This message focuses on the cost and the call of the cross of Christ. This message is especially appropriate as a part of a Good Friday service. To reinforce the power of the message, Communion is recommended.

KEY VERSE
"For you know that it was not with perishable things such as silver or gold that you were redeemed from the empty way of life handed down to you from your forefathers, but with the precious blood of Christ, a lamb without blemish or defect." 1 Peter 1:18-19

BIBLICAL BASIS
Isaiah 6:1-8; Matthew 27:28-31; Mark 8:34-38; John 6:47; 1 Corinthians 11:23-29; Colossians 2:13-15; 1 Peter 1:18-19

THE BIG IDEA
The cry of the Cross is to remember the cost and to answer the call.

PREPARATION
- *The Jesus Film* video (Inspirational Films, 1980)
- A TV and a VCR

Cue the video to the Crucifixion scene. (Note: Be prepared to show the video clip at the beginning of your message without an introduction. It is most effective after a solid time of worship and praise.)

Outline

THE CRY OF THE CROSS

The Big Idea
The cry of the Cross is to remember the cost and to answer the call.

INTRODUCTION

Show the Crucifixion clip; then ask students to think about the following question: **We know the scene, we see what Jesus went through, but do we really understand the cost?**

Do we understand the call the Cross has on our lives?

BODY OF THE MESSAGE

The cost of our salvation was so high that only Jesus' sacrifice on the cross could pay it.

I. Remember the Cost—Colossians 2:13-15

   A. God forgave all our sins, destroyed the charges against us, through the Cross.
      1. The Cross stands as a symbol of our sin and the price that needed to be paid.
      2. Read 1 Peter 1:19. Our salvation, our new life, came at the cost of His blood.
   B. Read Matthew 27:28-31. This is a graphic picture of the cost Jesus paid for us.
   C. Read John 6:47. Jesus came to Earth with one single focus: to go to the cross to give us *everlasting* life. Without Christ and the cross, our lives are empty and hollow.
   D. The Cross came with a *cost*, but it also comes with a *call*.
   E. Being a Christian doesn't mean knowing our Savior died on the cross for us and then going back to living our lives the way we want. Christianity is all about God and how we should live in surrender to Him and His glory.

II. Answer the Call—Mark 8:34-38

A. Jesus calls us to deny ourselves and take up our cross daily.
   1. Jesus is calling us to join Him in the cost—to suffer and surrender ourselves.
   2. The source of our salvation includes a call to suffer and surrender.
   3. In dying on the cross, Jesus bids us to come and die along with Him, to surrender our lives to Him.

Consider This

Thomas á Kempis (1380-1471), author of the Christian devotional classic *The Imitation of Christ*, wrote the following words about the contrast between those who profess to follow Christ and those who *really* follow Him:

"Jesus has many lovers of His heavenly kingdom, but few of them carry the cross. He has many friends who ask for consolation, but few who pray for affliction. He has many companions to share his meals, but few to share His abstinence. We all want to rejoice with Him, but few of us are willing to suffer anything for His sake. Many follow Jesus up to the breaking of the bread, but few go on to the drinking of the chalice of His passion."[1]

B. We want to follow Jesus as long as we're comfortable in doing so.
C. We've made God into "god"— we call the shots and He serves our needs and desires.
D. The Cross gave us such an incredible salvation, one that should leave us in awe and amazement of God, that we should be willing to lay down our lives for the One who laid His life down for us.
E. Jesus didn't die to give us life on our terms. He died to save us from our sin. We should be brought to our knees in surrender to the life we really need!

Consider This

Dietrich Bonhoeffer (1906-1945), Lutheran pastor and one of the few Christians who resisted Nazism in Germany instead of compromising with it, wrote: "Costly Grace . . . It is costly because it costs a man his life, and it is grace because it gives a man the only true life."[2]

CHALLENGE/ACTION STEPS

1. As long as you see the Cross only for what it gives us and not what it costs us, we will always experience only a taste of the real life that Jesus offers. Ask yourself the following questions:

- *Have I really understood the suffering, the sacrifice and the cost of what Jesus went through on the cross?*
- *Have I really heard the call of the Cross? Have I heard the call to join Jesus and surrender my very life to Him?*

2. Communion celebrates what Jesus has done for us.
   - Remember the cost: Sense anew the wonder and amazement of what God has done for each of us.
   - Answer the call: Make today the day that we surrender ourselves completely to Him. Read Isaiah 6:1-8. It was only after Isaiah saw God in all His holiness and glory that he could say in full surrender, "Here am I. Send me!" (verse 8).

Consider This

Thomas á Kempis imagined Jesus' words to believers:

"With my hands outstretched on the cross and My body naked, I willingly offered Myself to God the Father for your sins. Everything in Me was taken up in that sacrifice of divine propitiation. In like manner, you must willingly offer yourself to Me as a pure and holy oblation, with your whole heart and soul, and as lovingly as you can. I ask nothing less of you but that you endeavor to resign yourself completely to Me. Whatever else you offer Me besides yourself does not interest Me: I do not seek your gift, what I seek is you."[3]

PRAYER

This is what we celebrate today: His blood poured out and His body broken for each one of us.

COMMUNION

Explain and reflect on 1 Corinthians 11:23-29 as you serve Communion; then pray and dismiss by saying: **Leave in an attitude of reflection and silence—to return on Sunday joyful in celebration of the risen Lord.**

> **Note:** Due to Communion at the end of the message, no discussion starters are given for this study.

Notes
1. Thomas á Kempis, *The Imitation of Christ* (New York: Vintage Spiritual Classics, 1984), p. 63.
2. Dietrich Bonhoeffer, *The Cost of Discipleship* (New York: Collier Books, 1959), p. 47.
3. Thomas á Kempis, *The Imitation of Christ*, p. 195.

Overview

Surviving Your Family

TOPIC
Family

DESCRIPTION
None of us really has a choice regarding who our families are, but we do have a choice in how we will react to our families and the impact we can have on them. God gave us our families for a reason. That reason may be very clear for some; others may not see it at all. Instead of retreating from our families, we can choose to have a lasting, eternal impact on them for the kingdom of God.

KEY VERSE
"These commandments that I give you today are to be upon your hearts. Impress them on your children. Talk about them when you sit at home and when you walk along the road, when you lie down and when you get up." Deuteronomy 6:6-7

BIBLICAL BASIS
Deuteronomy 6:6-7; Psalm 139:13-16; Jeremiah 32:18; 2 Corinthians 5:17-20

THE BIG IDEA
God wants to use us to have a positive impact on our families.

PREPARATION
- A video camera and a blank videocassette
- A TV and a VCR

Preparation Option 1—Create a three- to five-minute Families video montage of TV families (e.g., *The Brady Bunch, Ozzie and Harriet, Leave It to Beaver, Everybody Loves Raymond, 7th Heaven, The Flintstones, The Jetsons, The Simpsons,* etc.) by taping the opening of the shows where the families are introduced via music, etc.

Preparation Option 2—Create a three- to five-minute Word-on-the-Street candid interview video by asking some students to share their thoughts on the following questions:

1. If you could describe your family in one word, what would it be?
2. What is the best thing about your family?
3. If you could change one thing about your family, what would it be?

Outline

SURVIVING YOUR FAMILY

> **The Big Idea**
> God wants to use us to have a positive impact on our families.

INTRODUCTION

Show the video prepared for option 1 or 2; then explain: **Every family struggles at times; it's what we do and how we react that can make all the difference in the world.**

No two families are alike and no family is perfect.

BODY OF THE MESSAGE

If we are ready to answer the call to make a difference for Christ in our families, there are three truths to keep in mind.

I. Our Families Impact Who We Are—Deuteronomy 6:6-7

A. Good or bad, our families impact us!

B. Read Deuteronomy 6:6-7 and Jeremiah 32:18. Our families directly affect us.

1. Our families impact our values, what we think about and believe in.

2. Our families impact how we treat others because of the way we're treated.

C. Each person's family is the main example of what a family is like.

1. For some, our families are great: supportive, nurturing, encouraging and loving.

2. For some, our families aren't so great: divorced, angry, harsh and cold.

II. Our Families Are Gifts from God—Psalm 139:13-16

A. Some of us may be thinking about our families: *Thanks but no thanks, God!*

B. God places a high value on family.

1. God placed us in our families.

2. God knows all about our families—good and bad.

3. God cares about what's going on in our families.

C. God gave us our families for a reason.

1. Some of us were given a great family to be nurtured by.

2. Some of us were given a chance to see what a family shouldn't be.

a. Our family circumstances can bring us to a relationship with Christ.

b. God can use us as lights—agents of change—in our families.

III. Our Families Can Be a Place Where We Can Make a Difference—2 Corinthians 5:17-20

A. We can make a difference in the lives of the people we love.

1. We can act as ambassadors for Christ in our families.

2. By being brothers and sisters in Christ, we can make a difference in the lives of our friends who don't have a great family.

B. Read 2 Corinthians 5:17-20. The only way we can be agents of change in our family—or in someone else's—is to first know our need for Jesus Christ!

1. The only way to see our family impacted is to first have our lives changed by Christ.

2. Jesus is the place to start. Without Him the pieces won't fit into place.

CHALLENGE/ACTION STEPS

God wants to use us to impact our families, but there are a few choices we need to make first.

- Choose to make Jesus first in your life.
- Choose to accept your family the way it is.
- Choose to do whatever it takes to be an agent of change.

SURVIVING YOUR FAMILY

1. If you could describe your family in one word, what would it be?

2. What is the best thing about your family?

3. If you could change one thing about your family, what would it be?

4. What is your reaction to the following three truths? Which is the easiest for you to see? Which is the hardest?

   • Choose to make Jesus first in your life.
   • Choose to accept your family the way it is.
   • Choose to do whatever it takes to be an agent of change.

5. What are three action steps you can begin taking to strengthen your family and be an agent of positive change?

Overview

THE FREEDOM OF FORGIVENESS

TOPIC
Forgiveness

DESCRIPTION
Forgiveness can be one of the hardest things to do in the entire world, yet it is a character quality that we are called to by God. We are called to forgive just as God has forgiven us—to the same extent and with the same depth that was offered to us. This message explores concrete ways in which to forgive others and experience the freedom that can come from authentically forgiving.

KEY VERSE
"Bear with each other and forgive whatever grievances you may have against one another. Forgive as the Lord forgave you." Colossians 3:13

BIBLICAL BASIS
Psalm 103:10,12; Micah 7:19; Matthew 5:44; Romans 8:28-29; Galatians 6:1-2; Ephesians 4:32; Colossians 2:13-14; 3:13; 1 John 1:9

THE BIG IDEA
As Christians, we're called to forgive others as God has forgiven us.

PREPARATION
• Copies of "Challenge/Action Steps" (p. 53)

Outline

THE FREEDOM OF FORGIVENESS

The Big Idea
As Christians, we're called to forgive others as God has forgiven us.

INTRODUCTION

Explain: **Everyone has been hurt. Maybe someone stabbed you with hurtful words. Maybe someone claimed to love you only to use you. Maybe someone said he or she would never leave you and then did it anyway. Maybe you've even been verbally or physically abused.**

Consider This

The year was 1947. It was almost two full years after the liberation of Auschwitz, as Corrie ten Boom stepped forward to share the message of forgiveness and healing at a German church. As she stepped forward, she prayed that God would use her words to bring about healing, forgiveness and restoration. What she was about to experience changed her life forever.

As she finished her message, a man stepped forward, moving his way through the crowd of people to talk to Corrie. He looked familiar, like she'd seen him somewhere before. As she looked into his eyes, it all become crystal clear. She recognized him and remembered the uniform . . . the whips . . . walking past him naked at the selection. She remembered her sister dying a slow and painful death at his hands. The memories came flooding back to her . . . memories from Auschwitz and this man who had been a guard at the camp.

"I'm a Christian now." He spoke with his eyes sadly looking into hers. "I know that God has forgiven me, but will *you* forgive me?" He stretched out his hand to receive hers.

She stood there for what must have seemed an eternity, although it was probably only a moment or two. She knew that she needed to make a choice. Would she forgive the man at whose hand she experienced so much hurt, pain and humiliation? Would she? Could she?

"Jesus, I need Your help. I can lift my hand, but You need to supply the

---

feeling." She slowly raised her hand, reached out to the man and took his hand in hers. As she reached out, a warm sensation filled her heart. God was indeed faithful. "I forgive you, brother—with my whole heart!"

That day, former guard and former prisoner were both healed and set free from the bondage of bitterness and anger.[1]

Pain runs deep, but there is a deeper pain—the inability to forgive.

BODY OF THE MESSAGE

In forgiving others, we have to *know*, *go* and *show*.

I. *Know* How Much God Has Forgiven Us—Colossians 2:13-14

A. God forgave us wholly and completely through Christ's sacrifice on the cross.
   1. God forgives everyone, for everything, every time.
   2. There is nothing that God cannot or would not forgive. No sin is too great or too small for God.
B. God forgave us unconditionally.
   1. Read Psalm 103:12. God's forgiveness is true forgiveness—once He forgives us, we are forever forgiven. God's forgiveness doesn't say "Today, I'll forgive you, but tomorrow . . ."
   2. Read Micah 7:19. There are no strings attached to God's forgiveness. God doesn't play "If . . . then" games when it comes to forgiving us.
C. God forgave us before we even asked.
   1. God took the first step toward us.
   2. God chose to forgive us, even before we asked for it!
   3. God offers forgiveness as a gift to us.

II. *Go* and Forgive As God Has Forgiven Us—Ephesians 4:32

A. Read Psalm 103:10. We should remember that God forgives us, even though we don't deserve it.
B. We all want to be forgiven.
   1. Read Ephesians 4:32. The phrase "just as" is telling us that we are to forgive to the same depth and extent that God forgives us.
   2. Because we call ourselves Christians, we need to forgive others to the same extent that we want Jesus to forgive us.
C. Do we forgive completely, unconditionally and immediately?
   1. How can we expect God to forgive us any differently than how we choose to forgive others?

2. Are we any better than anyone else? Is someone else's sin worse than ours?

III. *Show* Forgiveness by the Choices We Make—Colossians 3:13

A. Forgiveness is a choice—it is an act of our free will.
   1. Forgiveness is a choice to give to others what we have received from God.
   2. It is a choice that will free us from bondage, bitterness and pain.
B. There are four choices that we need to make in order to forgive someone.
   1. We must choose to live with the consequences.
      a. Forgiveness is choosing to live with the consequences of someone else's actions, regardless of how much they hurt us.
      b. Consequences hurt; just ask God how much it hurt to forgive us!
      c. The first step of forgiveness is asking ourselves, *Can I live with the consequences?*
   2. We must choose to leave the past behind.
      a. Forgiveness is a choice to not hold on to the sin or the past.
      b. It doesn't mean holding on to the hurt until we can get even.
      c. It does mean choosing not to live or be haunted by the past anymore.
   3. We must choose to let others off our hook.
      a. Forgiveness is an act of faith; it shows that we believe God is a better judge than we are *and* that His justice is better than ours.
      b. Forgiving means giving up our right to seek revenge.
      c. Forgiveness is letting go and allowing God to deal with the person.
   4. We must choose to lift the bondage we are in—to be freed from the weight of holding on to our pain and anger.
      a. When we forgive, we are released from the pain and heartache.
      b. Forgiving heals us and heals the person who wronged us. Imagine the freedom that Corrie ten Boom and the former guard received.

> **Suggestion**
> Check out *Victory over the Darkness*[2] or *Stomping Out the Darkness*[3] for help in answering the question, What do you do if the person who hurt you is unrepentant and continues to hurt you?

CHALLENGE/ACTION STEPS

Use the following steps, adapted from *Stomping Out the Darkness*, to begin forgiving those who've hurt you:[4]

> **Note:** These forgiveness steps need to be done in private or with a counselor—not in a group setting.

1. List the names of people who've hurt you and what they did that hurt you.

2. Face the hurt and the hate that you feel toward the people you listed. Write down how you feel about them and what they did to you. Remember, you can't hide how you feel from God—He already knows.

3. Realize that the cross of Christ not only makes forgiveness possible but also fair and right. Jesus took upon Himself all the sins of the world—including those who have hurt you.

4. Decide that you will bear the burden of each person's sin (see Galatians 6:1-2). Accepting the fact that you will live with the consequences of what was done means that you will not seek revenge, hold it against the other person or use it against them.

5. Consciously make the decision to forgive. You may not feel like forgiving, but God does not call us to do anything He won't equip us to do. He will give you the strength to forgive—even when you don't feel like it.

6. Realize that forgiveness does not condone another's sin; it doesn't mean that you are saying that what was done is okay. Instead, it releases the burden of dealing with the sin to God.

7. Pray the following prayer aloud for each person on your list: "I forgive (name) for (list the offense)." Take your time in dealing with each person and each offense, and allow God to work in your heart for each situation.

8. Destroy the list. You don't need to tell those you've forgiven what you have done—forgiveness is a matter of your heart and is between you and God.

9. Do not expect that your decision to forgive will result in major changes in those you forgive. Pray for those who've wronged you (see Matthew 5:44) so that they may find the freedom of forgiveness.

10. Expect positive results of forgiveness in *you*. In time, you will be able to think about the other person without feeling hurt, angry or bitter.

11. Thank God for the lessons you've learned and the maturity you've gained as a result of your decision to forgive the offenders (see Romans 8:28-29).

12. Be sure to accept your part of the blame. Confess anything you need to (see 1 John 1:9). If you need to go to someone to ask for forgiveness—go for it!

Notes

1. Jim Burns and Greg McKinnon, *Illustrations, Stories and Quotes* (Ventura, CA: Gospel Light, 1997), pp. 179-180.
2. Neil T. Anderson, *Victory over the Darkness* (Ventura, CA: Regal Books, 2000).
3. Neil T. Anderson and Dave Park, *Stomping Out the Darkness* (Ventura, CA: Regal Books, 1993).
4. Ibid., pp. 176-178.

THE FREEDOM OF FORGIVENESS

1. Why is forgiveness so difficult with certain people?

2. What are the consequences of not forgiving others?

3. What are the benefits of forgiving others?

4. Who are you finding it difficult to forgive? Why?

Overview

GOD'S AMAZING GRACE

TOPIC
God's grace

DESCRIPTION
Our world is desperate for grace. It is desperate to know love and value that stands outside of performance and accomplishments. We all experience sin in our lives, but what we desperately need to receive is the same thing we are called to give away—grace. This message explores the depth of God's grace for us and the need to offer it as freely as we have received it.

KEY VERSE
"'Then neither do I condemn you,' Jesus declared. 'Go now and leave your life of sin.'" John 8:11

BIBLICAL BASIS
John 2:4; 8:1-11; 19:26; Romans 3:21-26; 6:1-2,23; 8:38-39; Ephesians 2:4-9

THE BIG IDEA
Grace is a gift we desperately need to receive *and* give.

PREPARATION
- The *Les Miserables* video (Columbia TriStar, 1997)
- A TV and a VCR

Cue the video to the first scenes just after the opening credits, showing Jean Valjean (played by Liam Neeson) in a town square. You'll end the clip with Jean Valjean staring at the bishop after his speech.

Outline

GOD'S AMAZING GRACE

> **The Big Idea**
> Grace is a gift we desperately need to receive *and* give.

INTRODUCTION

Show the clip from *Les Miserables*. Afterward, explain: **Our world is desperate for grace. But just what is grace exactly and why are we so desperate to receive it?**

BODY OF THE MESSAGE

John 8:1-11 is one of the most incredible encounters with Jesus in all of Scripture and one that defines the gift of grace. There are four life-changing truths about grace.

I. Grace Is a Gift We Don't Deserve—John 8:1-3

A. Refer to John 2:4; 19:26. "Woman" is the term of honor and respect that Jesus used when He was talking to His mother. Read John 8:10-11. Jesus used the same term to address the adulteress, even though, according to the culture, she didn't deserve the honor and respect it showed.

B. God's grace is something we desperately need but don't deserve.

   1. Jesus knew all about the woman's sin, but He also saw beneath the layers of pain and humiliation.

   2. We all want forgiveness, acceptance and love.

C. Read Romans 6:23 and Ephesians 2:4-9. God should condemn us; instead, He gives His love, forgiveness, mercy, healing and honor.

II. Grace Is a Gift That Doesn't Make Sense—John 8:11

A. Jesus sent the woman away without condemnation. Grace *is* irrational; it's not what we deserve.

   1. God's unconditional love for us is completely independent of what we do.

      a. Read Ephesians 2:8-9. We can't do anything to make God love us any more than He already does.

      b. Read Romans 8:38-39. There is nothing we can do that will cause God to stop loving us.

      c. God's love is not based on what we do but who we are.

2. God's forgiveness is not dependent on our worthiness—it is undeserved.
   a. God's forgiveness is offered to everyone, for anything and at any time.
   b. We need and desire God's forgiveness.

III. Grace Is a Gift That Is Life Transforming—John 8:11

A. In His love, Jesus not only gave the woman grace, but He also refused to leave her to live her life in the manner she had been living it.

B. When we truly encounter the amazing grace of God, we can't help but be changed and transformed.
   1. We are changed from the inside out.
      a. Read Romans 6:1-2. When we encounter the grace of God, we are changed. We are no longer slaves to sin but have the freedom to live our lives as He intended for us.
      b. God's grace and forgiveness change our hearts and leads to repentance.
   2. We are transformed into agents of grace.
      a. Not only are we changed within, but we are also able to extend grace freely wherever we go. We begin to give away the very grace we have received from God: forgiving others, accepting others and loving others as He does.
      b. Unfortunately, the Church is known more as a dispenser of judgment than as a dispenser of grace. Too often Christians play the part of the Pharisees in the lives of others—swift to judge, slow to give grace—rather than acting the way Jesus would.

IV. Grace Is a Gift with a Price Tag—Romans 3:21-26

A. Read Romans 3:24. God's amazing grace had a high price, paid for by Jesus with His own blood on the cross.

B. Romans 3:25-26 gives us a glimpse of the price that was paid. In Jesus Christ, God the Father provided for us the grace we desperately need and search for—and absolutely don't deserve.

CHALLENGE/ACTION STEPS

1. Think about the things you've done that have put you far away from receiving God's grace; then receive His amazing grace as the gift He wants to give you.
2. Are you like the Pharisees? Are you swift to judge and slow to give grace?
3. Consciously work this week to freely give away God's grace to others. It will change your life from the inside out.

GOD'S AMAZING GRACE

1. What words would you use to define the word "grace"?

2. How have you experienced God's grace in your life?

3. Why is it difficult to receive God's grace in our lives?

4. Why is it difficult to give away God's grace to others?

5. Who do you relate to: the woman caught in the act of adultery or the Pharisees?

6. What is one action step you need to do because of what you've heard today?

Overview

PLUGGING IN TO THE POWER SOURCE

TOPIC
The Holy Spirit

DESCRIPTION
Jesus has left us a power source in the person of the Holy Spirit. He is all the power we need to live the Christian life. We have all the power, but the question is, Do we plug into that power every day? This message explores four roles of the Holy Spirit in the life of every believer and how to plug in to that source of power.

KEY VERSE
"But I tell you the truth: It is for your good that I am going away. Unless I go away, the Counselor will not come to you; but if I go, I will send him to you." John 16:7

BIBLICAL BASIS
John 14:12; 16:5-15; Ephesians 4:30; 5:18

THE BIG IDEA
As Christians, God gives us the Holy Spirit, but do we plug in to His power?

PREPARATION
- A blender (and extension cord, if needed)
- Small paper cups
- Milk
- Vanilla ice cream
- Chocolate syrup

Outline

PLUGGING IN TO THE POWER SOURCE

> **The Big Idea**
> As Christians, God gives us the Holy Spirit, but do we plug in to His power?

INTRODUCTION

Sometimes as Christians, our lives seem to lack power and vitality. We try to do all the right things, but we seem to lack something. We turn around and think, *Is this all there really is to Christianity?*

Object Lesson Option 1

As you add each milkshake ingredient into the *unplugged* blender, describe one thing we can do to know God better (e.g., pray, study the Bible, worship, etc.). After you've added all the necessary ingredients, push a button to start blending—nothing will happen. Hold up the power cord and explain: **Just because we have all the right ingredients to make an awesome milkshake doesn't mean we've done all we need to do to make one.**

Plug in the blender and push a button to start blending. After a moment, stop and explain: **Knowing God is like this too—we add all the right ingredients to our lives, but we forget to plug in to God's power source, the Holy Spirit. The Holy Spirit is there, but the question is, Do we choose to plug in to the power that could be ours?** Finish blending the milkshake and don't forget to share!

Object Lesson Option 2

Turn out all the lights in the room and explain: **Just like our lighting system has all it needs to function and do its job, it doesn't work by itself. The power is there, but we need to flip the switch to access it. We have all the power we need in our lives through the Holy Spirit, but do we plug in and do we turn it on?**

What does the Holy Spirit do in our lives and how do we plug in to His power?

BODY OF THE MESSAGE

In John 16:5-15, Jesus showed the disciples the four roles of the Holy Spirit.

I. The Holy Spirit Comforts—John 16:5-7

A. Read John 16:6-7. The Holy Spirit is our comforter. The Holy Spirit brings comfort in our lives when we are at our deepest need.

B. When we feel that God is with us in a tangible way, it is because of the ministry of the Holy Spirit in our lives.

II. The Holy Spirit Convicts—John 16:8-11

The Holy Spirit is sent to convict: past, present and future.

1. Read John 16:9. Past: We are convicted of the sin in our lives.
2. Read John 16:10. Present: We are shown where we need to live—in righteousness—and where we're falling short.
3. Read John 16:11. Future: We are warned of the coming judgment of God on this world.

III. The Holy Spirit Guides—John 16:12-13

A. Read John 16:13. The Holy Spirit will guide us "into all truth."
   1. He will guide us in what we should do and where we should go.
   2. He will bring to mind the words of Jesus and of Scripture.

B. Life can be tough; we need all the help we can get. The Holy Spirit is there to help us through this thing called life.

C. If we are in danger of following the wrong course, the Holy Spirit is available to point out the way we should go.

IV. The Holy Spirit Glorifies—John 16:14-15

A. Read John 16:14. The Holy Spirit glorifies Jesus Christ by giving to us from Jesus Himself.

B. Read John 16:15. The Holy Spirit gives us God's power so that we can have ministry in the lives of others. By giving to us and using us, the Holy Spirit makes sure that Jesus Christ is glorified in our world. He is the central focus, not us or anyone else.

C. Read John 14:12. We are told we will do "even greater things" than Jesus did when we follow Him. Through the power of the Holy Spirit, believers will continue the ministry Jesus had here on Earth, to continue what He has begun.

D. Read Ephesians 5:18. "Be filled with the Spirit." We are called to surrender to His reign in our lives every day.

CHALLENGE/ACTION STEPS

1. Get Ready! Look into your heart.
   - Am I plugged in to the power source?
   - Am I experiencing the four roles of the Holy Spirit in my life?
   - Is there anything in my life that could be clogging the power source?
2. Get Set! Act on what you learn about yourself.
   - Is there anything I need to confess?
   - Is there anything I need to surrender?
   - Is there someone I need to forgive?
   - Is there an attitude I need to change?
   - Is there a relationship I need to mend?
3. Go! Use what you know.
   - Read Ephesians 4:30. Do you confess your sins daily?
   - Read Ephesians 5:18. Do you surrender to God daily, yielding your life to the Holy Spirit to be used and molded?
   - Do you cling to Christ through His Word and in prayer?

PLUGGING IN TO THE POWER SOURCE

1. Why might some people feel unfulfilled in their relationship with God?

2. What is the source of true fulfillment in a relationship with God?

3. In which of the four roles—comforter, convicter, guide, glorifier of Jesus—do you see the Holy Spirit most clearly in your life?

4. Which of the four roles do you see Him in the least?

5. Read Ephesians 4:30. What are some ways in which we can "grieve the Holy Spirit"?

6. What is one thing blocking the power source of the Holy Spirit in your life?

7. What are three action steps you can take this week to plug in to the power of the Holy Spirit?

Overview

WHO DO YOU LISTEN TO?

TOPIC
Influences

DESCRIPTION
Whether it's through the radio, TV, the Internet or movies, we are bombarded every day with a myriad of mixed messages. Messages about our worth, our value and our fulfillment come from every direction. This message gives students practical tools to be able to discern what messages and influences they are listening to and the impact those messages have.

KEY VERSE
"See to it that no one takes you captive through hollow and deceptive philosophy, which depends on human tradition and the basic principles of this world rather than on Christ." Colossians 2:8

BIBLICAL BASIS
Romans 12:1-2; Colossians 2:6-8; 3:1-4; 1 Thessalonians 5:21

THE BIG IDEA
Every day we make a choice about who we are going to listen to and believe.

PREPARATION
- A TV and a VCR
- A video camera and a blank videocassette

Create a 5- to 10-minute video montage of the most popular commercials on television.

Outline

WHO DO YOU LISTEN TO?

The Big Idea
Every day we make a choice about who we are going to listen to and believe.

INTRODUCTION

Show the video montage; then transition to the message by explaining: **We are bombarded with messages every day—messages meant to move, change and challenge us. What we think, value and do in life is influenced by the messages we're exposed to.**

Who you listen to will mold and shape you.

BODY OF THE MESSAGE

There are three choices we need to make concerning who we listen to.

I. Don't Be Led Astray—Colossians 2:6-8

A. Read Colossians 2:8. Don't be led astray by empty and hollow messages.
   1. There are a lot of messages that promise something but don't deliver.
      a. Advertising says: If you have this or look like this, then you'll be happy, significant and have value.
      b. TV and movies teach that happiness is found through wealth, power and physical satisfaction.
   2. Remember: What you see isn't always what you get.
B. Read Colossians 2:6-7. God calls us to be focused on Christ.

II. Don't Be Conformed, But Be Changed—Romans 12:1-2

A. "Do not conform any longer to the pattern of this world" (Romans 12:2).
   1. Live as an original.
   2. Sometimes we strive so hard to be accepted that we become a carbon copy of someone else and lose our true identity.
B. Being conformed means being pressed into a mold of what we hear.

1. When we buy into these messages we hear, they mold us.

C. God challenges us to not be conformed but instead to be changed and molded by Him.

D. As you walk with God and look to Him, you'll see that your life, attitudes and values will begin to change to be more like His.

III. Don't Settle for Less Than the Real Thing—Colossians 3:1-4

A. When we buy into hollow and empty messages, we settle for cheap imitations of real life.

B. Read Colossians 3:3. We should seek Christ in order to find the truth for our lives.

C. Read Colossians 3:1-4. We are to ignore temporal messages and seek Jesus in our hearts.

CHALLENGE/ACTION STEPS

First Thessalonians 5:21 warns us to "test everything." Give yourself the following T-E-S-T:

T—Is it *true* and *trustworthy*?

E—Is it *edifying* to others?

S—Is it *seen* in God's Word?

T—Is it a *trap*? Is it enslaving?

WHO DO YOU LISTEN TO?

1. List some of the messages that bombard us every day and the influence they have on our world.

2. Do these messages pass the T-E-S-T?
   T—Is it *true* and *trustworthy*?
   E—Is it *edifying* to others?
   S—Is it *seen* in God's Word?
   T—Is it a *trap*? Is it enslaving?

3. List some of the messages that are powerful in your life.

4. Do these messages pass the T-E-S-T?

5. List some messages we should be filling our lives with.

6. What steps can we take to fill our lives with God's messages?

Overview

THERMOSTAT OR THERMOMETER?

TOPIC
Being a person of influence

DESCRIPTION
As we live our daily lives, will we be influenced by those around us or will we influence them instead? This message seeks to give students practical ways in which to live above the world's influence every day.

KEY VERSE
"Do not conform any longer to the pattern of this world, but be transformed by the renewing of your mind. Then you will be able to test and approve what God's will is—his good, pleasing and perfect will." Romans 12:2

BIBLICAL BASIS
Psalm 25:4-5; Proverbs 24:21; 27:17; John 15:4; Romans 5:4; 12:1-2; 1 Corinthians 15:33

THE BIG IDEA
We can either live under the influence or above the influence; the choice is ours to make.

PREPARATION
- A banana
- A large piece of aluminum foil

Outline

THERMOSTAT OR THERMOMETER?

> **The Big Idea**
> We can either live under the influence or above the influence; the choice is ours to make.

INTRODUCTION

Think about a personal illustration concerning a time when you felt the pressure to conform and you did. Share your story; then transition to the message by pointing out that we do one of two things: We are either influenced by others, or we are an influence on others; i.e., we either live under the influence or above the influence.

> **Consider This**
> Living under the influence means
> - Being involved in something only because others are.
> - Seeking to be liked and accepted, being scared of rejection.
> - Worrying about what others might think or say.
>
> The results of living under the influence are
> - Trading who we really are for a cheap imitation.
> - Living a lie by acting like someone we're really not.
> - Thinking we're being independent while actually living under the influence of others.

BODY OF THE MESSAGE

Whether we choose to live under the influence or above the influence, there are three truths to consider.

I. We Are Influenced by the Company We Keep— 1 Corinthians 15:33

   A. "Do not be misled: 'Bad company corrupts good character'" (1 Corinthians 15:33).
   - "Do not join with the rebellious" (Proverbs 24:21). We become like the people we spend time with.

   B. "Remain in me, and I will remain in you" (John 15:4). The more time we spend in God's company the more Christlike we become.

II. We Must Choose Our Relationships Wisely

A. We need to carefully consider who we should spend time with.

1. *Do I want to be like this person?*

2. *Does this person honor God with his or her life?*

3. *Do I want this person to have an influence on my life?*

B. We should keep our attention continually focused on God's will for our lives.

III. We Can Either Reflect Our Surroundings or Set Them

A. We can act as thermometers or thermostats.

1. Thermometers reflect the temperature; they're influenced by surroundings.

2. Thermostats set the temperature, influencing their surroundings.

B. Our relationships are indicators of our status as thermometers or thermostats.

1. Following someone else's lead and acting as a thermometer is always easy.

2. We are called to be thermostats and to influence others for Christ.

C. If we want to live above the influence and be a thermostat for God, we will need to set the P-A-C-E.

1. **P**—We need to change our *perspective.*

a. Read Romans 12:1-2. Don't simply copy others. Let God transform you.

b. It is a choice to change the way we think and live and who influences us. It is a complete change of perspective.

c. We do not need to conform, copying the behavior and customs of other; we need to be transformed—completely changed by God.

Object Lesson

Take the aluminum foil and mold it around the banana. Carefully slide the banana out, leaving the aluminum shell. Transition by explaining: **Although the shell has the shape of the banana, there's no way it can ever be a real banana—it's a cheap and unfulfilling imitation of the real thing. When we choose to be conformed, or molded, by the values and attitudes of the world, we fall into the trap of becoming a hollow and empty shell of whom God has created us to be. That's the change of perspective.**

---

2. **A**—We need to *allow* God's influence on our lives.
   a. Psalm 25:4-5. We need to choose to allow God to be our main influence.
   b. It's often easier to live your life to please your parents, your friends, your boyfriend or girlfriend, but what about God? He is the One we should live to please.
   c. Living to please and glorify God is tough in today's world.
      • It requires choosing to find worth in God, not in what we do or what others around us think.
      • God's love is based on who we are, not what we do.
   d. We must choose daily to seek to please God instead of those around us. It is a daily choice to ask, "God, what would you have me do?"

3. **C**—We need to have *consistent character*.
   a. Read Romans 5:4. Living consistently builds up our character.
   b. Character is what we do and who we are when no one is watching. Being a thermostat means choosing to live life consistently, even when others aren't watching.
   c. We should live our lives as if our every move is being videotaped.
      • Is your life really consistent?
      • Would you act and react the same way regardless of who you were around?
   d. Having consistent character impacts others.
      • Others will see that our lives are different or transformed.
      • Others will be inspired to change.

4. **E**—We should *encourage* others.
   a. Everyone needs encouragement.
   b. The power of encouragement is an incredible influence.
      • If we're encouragers, people will want to be around us.
      • Others are drawn to positive and encouraging people.
   c. "As iron sharpens iron, so one man sharpens another" (Proverbs 27:17).
      • We sharpen each other through encouragement.
      • Those who act as thermostats encourage others.
      • True friends sharpen each other by keeping one another's actions accountable.
   d. We should find ways to encourage those around us.

CHALLENGE/ACTION STEPS

P—Are you changing your *perspective*?

Where in your life are you being molded and not transformed?

A—Do you *allow* God to be your main influence?

Who are you living for? Who are you seeking to please?

C—Do you have *consistent character*?

What areas of your life are in conflict with consistency?

E—Do you *encourage* others?

Who in your life needs the power of encouragement?

What will you do about it this week?

THERMOSTAT OR THERMOMETER?

1. Has there ever been a time when you made a choice under the influence of someone else? What happened?

2. State 1 Corinthians 15:33 as if you were going to teach it to a group of children.

3. Read Romans 12:1-2. What do you think it means to be conformed into the pattern of the world?

4. What are some ways in which we can be transformed?

5. Read Romans 5:4. How would you define the word "character"?

6. Read Proverbs 27:17. What are some ways you can encourage others around you?

7. What is one thing you know you need to do because of what you heard today?

Overview

BECOMING A PERSON OF INTEGRITY

TOPIC
Integrity

DESCRIPTION
God is looking for people of integrity. This message examines the life of Joseph as a model of integrity. It explores what tests our integrity, as well as what commitments we need to make that will preserve our integrity.

KEY VERSE
"I looked for a man [or woman] among them who would build up the wall and stand before me in the gap on behalf of the land so I would not have to destroy it, but I found none." Ezekiel 22:30

BIBLICAL BASIS
Genesis 37:5-28; 39; 40:8,12-23; 50:19-21; Psalm 15; Ezekiel 22:30

THE BIG IDEA
God is looking for people of integrity—people He can use to make a difference.

PREPARATION
None

Outline

BECOMING A PERSON OF INTEGRITY

The Big Idea
God is looking for people of integrity—people He can use to make a difference.

INTRODUCTION

Divide students into discussion groups of three or four. If possible, assign an adult to each group as a facilitator. Pose the following questions and allow a few minutes for the small groups to discuss. If time allows, briefly discuss answers as a whole group.

1. What comes to mind when you think of the word "integrity"?
2. What are some things that challenge a person's integrity?
3. What are some areas in which we can lack integrity?

Consider This
Integrity is
    a battle against compromise,
    forged over a lifetime,
    tarnished in a moment, and
    a match between your words and your actions.

Joseph was a man who had an abundance of integrity.

BODY OF THE MESSAGE

From the life of Joseph, we can see three tests of integrity and four commitments people of integrity need to make.

THREE TESTS OF INTEGRITY

I. The Test of Adversity—Genesis 37:5-28

> **Consider This**
> Share an illustration from your life when God used adversity in your life to refine you to be more like Him or be a stronger person of integrity.

A. Read Genesis 39:8. Our convictions become clear when we are tested through adversity.

B. Adversity can test our faith. It is in tough times that God can refine us to be more like Him.

II. The Test of Prosperity—Genesis 39:1-5

A. Read Genesis 39:4. Prosperity can test our integrity. It's easy to have faith when all is going well, our lives are prosperous, and we feel no real need.

B. In the midst of our wealth, we are actually more needy. All the wealth in the world cannot buy happiness or integrity.

III. The Test of Contentment—Genesis 39:6

A. Read Genesis 40:23. When he was freed from jail, the chief cupbearer forgot Joseph. Being comfortable in life is a test of our integrity.

B. When all of our needs are met, it's easy for us to forget about God.

FOUR COMMITMENTS OF INTEGRITY

I. The Commitment of Purity—Genesis 39:6-18

A. In Genesis 39:9, Joseph made a commitment to remain pure in spite of temptation.

B. One of the greatest commitments we can make is to remain sexually pure.
  1. When we make a commitment to live a life of sexual purity, we show ourselves to be different.
  2. Lack of sexual purity shows a lack of integrity.

C. We need God's help to remain pure.

II. The Commitment of Attitude—Genesis 39:19-23

A. In Genesis 39:20-21, Joseph's commitment to have a good attitude in spite of his surroundings was tested as he was falsely imprisoned.

B. When we can't change our circumstance, we can still change our attitude.

C. A bad attitude can sink our integrity by leading us to say and do things that compromise our integrity in the eyes of others.

III. The Commitment of Faithfulness—Genesis 40:8,12-23

A. In Genesis 40:8, Joseph's commitment to be faithful, to do what was right in spite of no guarantee that it would better his circumstance, was tested. We are called to be faithful, even when it hurts or we aren't guaranteed a reward.

B. God wants us to be bound by our word—people of integrity.

C. We are called to walk in faithfulness, even when the circumstances make it hard.

IV. The Commitment of Consistency—Genesis 50:19-21

A. In Genesis 50:20, Joseph's commitment of consistency in spite of the conditions he had been forced to live under was also tested.

B. We should strive for consistency every day.

1. We should be known for our consistency and faithfulness.

2. Our lives must to be marked by consistency in order for us to be people of integrity.

CHALLENGE/ACTION STEPS

1. Which of the three tests are you currently experiencing?

2. Which of the four commitments do you need to take action on today?

3. Read Psalm 15 and use it as a prayer of integrity for yourself and your church.

BECOMING A PERSON OF INTEGRITY

1. How would you define the word "integrity"?

2. Why do we need to be people of integrity?

3. Why is it at times difficult to find people of integrity?

4. Why is it difficult to be a person of integrity?

5. Which of the three Tests of Integrity is the most difficult for you? Why?

6. Of the four Commitments of Integrity, which is the most difficult for you right now? Why?

7. What in your life needs to change, grow, be strengthened or thrown out so that you will be more of a person of integrity? What can others do to help?

8. As a group, pray about the needs discussed in question 7.

Overview

UNFATHOMABLE GOD

TOPIC
God's love for us

DESCRIPTION
God is the passionate lover of His people. This message highlights Jesus' parable of the lost son (or, better, the parable of the loving father), which explores the depth of the father's love for his son, even to the extent of restoring him to his place in the family after he had deserted it. The portrait is life changing as we encounter our loving God who is wildly, beautifully, unfathomably loving!

KEY VERSE
"But while he was still a long way off, his father saw him and was filled with compassion for him; he ran to his son, threw his arms around him and kissed him." Luke 15:20

BIBLICAL BASIS
Zephaniah 3:17; Luke 15:11-24

THE BIG IDEA
When we see God for who He really is and what He's done, we can't help but run to Him.

PREPARATION
Think of a personal illustration of a time when you had a get-me-out-of-this-one-and-I'll-do-anything-for-You! attitude and be prepared to share the experience with the group.

Outline

UNFATHOMABLE GOD

> **The Big Idea**
> When we see God for who He really is and what He's done, we can't help but run to Him.

INTRODUCTION

After telling the get-me-out-of-this-one-and-I'll-do-anything-for-You! life experience you prepared, explain: **All of us have probably prayed that at least once in our lives. But if you think about it, it's a misconception about God for us to think that He's there only to save us from ourselves. Some of us live with the thought,** *If I could go back and change just one thing, I'd change* _____ *but if God ever really found out . . .* **Too late—and impossible, to boot—God already knows everything about us, and He still seeks us in love.**

> **Consider This**
> Misconceptions About God
> 1. He's distant—"God doesn't know anything about what's going on; He's out *there* somewhere."
> 2. He's demanding—"God is just rules and regulations, always keeping score."
> 3. He's a deadbeat dad—"He didn't get me that new motorcycle I prayed so hard for."
> 4. He's distracted—"There's no way He knows or cares about me. He's too busy being God."

Don't treat God like a vending machine, where you put in your quarter, push the button and get what you want every time.

BODY OF THE MESSAGE

The Parable of the Lost Son is really more about the father and the incredible, unfathomable love that he had for his wayward son.

I. A Loving Father and a Selfish Son—Luke 15:11-13

A. Read Luke 15:12. A father honored his son's request for his inheritance to be given early.
   1. The son's request required incredible sacrifice and disgrace to the father. Honoring the request would publicly acknowledge that the son was better off with the father dead.
   2. The father loved his son so much that he was willing to pay the price of honoring his son's request.
   3. Sometimes our selfishness causes us to think only about what we need and not what's best for us.

B. Read Luke 15:13. The greedy son took everything and left, turning his back on his family.
   1. The son was sure that his surroundings—his circumstances—were keeping him from being happy.
      a. He traveled to a distant land searching for fulfillment.
      b. He was never content, always longing for something or someplace else.
   2. We can be so busy wanting what we don't have that we can't see or enjoy what we do have.

II. Trouble in Paradise—Luke 15:14-16

A. Read Luke 15:14. The young man wasted his inheritance and had nothing left over to feed himself when the famine came.
   1. He went from being a big spender to working in a field feeding pigs—unclean animals in the eyes of Jews—hoping someone would feed him. He had lived wildly through his wealth and now he was wishing he could share the pods the pigs ate.
   2. He realized that the paradise he had been looking for was not to be found. Things that appear too good to be true usually *are*.
   3. He had been the life of the party, known and loved while he had money.

B. His so-called friends were nowhere to be found in his time of need.

III. The Son Returns Home—Luke 15:17-19

A. God brought the young man to a place where he looked in the mirror.
   1. Sin blinds us to our condition, so we imagine that we are happy when in reality we are miserable.
   2. Miserable people have found what they thought would make them happy only to realize it doesn't—and then they try to convince themselves that they truly have it all.

B. God revealed to the son the depth to which he had fallen.

1. He realized where he was and what he really needed in life—to be back with his father.

2. He thought about what he would say when he arrived at his father's doorstep.

3. He was willing to become a hired man if only his father would take him back.

IV. The Father Embraces His Wayward Son—Luke 15:20-24

A. The father had spent many nights in anguish over his son's leaving.

B. He welcomed his son with open arms of compassion.

1. The father actually ran to meet his son. Once again, because of his love for his son, the father cast aside what others would think.

2. The son tried to tell his father that he was not worthy to be treated as a son. The father didn't lecture or reprimand; instead, he called for the best of everything to be showered upon his son in celebration of his returning.

3. We are loved even more by our heavenly Father than the prodigal son was loved by his earthly one. Our heavenly Father asks only that we return to Him, and He will run to meet us with open arms.

Consider This

The gifts showered upon the prodigal son by his father all have significance in the acceptance of the son and his restoration into the family.

- Robe—stood for the lost dignity; it was a robe given to a guest of honor.
- Ring—placed on the hand that squandered his wealth, it reinstated his authority over the family affairs.
- Sandals—represented the servant (field worker) that had become a free man again.
- Feast—served as a meal fit for a king (or an incredibly loved son).

CHALLENGE/ACTION STEPS

1. Turn to God and allow Him to welcome you into His open arms. Feel His love and compassion for you, no matter where you've been or what you've done.

2. Read Zephaniah 3:17. Consider your sin and realize there is nothing too big or too small for God to forgive.

UNFATHOMABLE GOD

1. With which of the four misconceptions about God can you identify and why?

2. What other misconceptions about God can you think of?

3. Finish the following sentence: If I could go back in time and change just one thing, I'd change . . .

4. What do you think or how do you feel about God being insanely in love with you, enough to forgive you for anything, anytime?

5. Why is it so hard at times to see God as our loving Father?

6. Has there ever been a time when you could really relate to the prodigal son in the parable?

7. In what ways could the truth and reality of God's love change the way we live our lives?

8. Spend some time in prayer, thanking God for His love and expressing to Him whatever you feel.

Overview

WHAT'S LOVE GOT TO DO WITH IT?

TOPIC
Loving others

DESCRIPTION
As Christians, we are called to love one another. Jesus made that very clear. It is one of the defining marks of a follower of Him. In this message, we survey the book of 1 John to see what it means to truly love one another. The aim of the message is to help our students discover the impact of their love for one another, as well as discover how simple it is to give away Christlike love.

KEY VERSE
"Anyone who claims to be in the light but hates his brother is still in the darkness. Whoever loves his brother lives in the light, and there is nothing in him to make him stumble." 1 John 2:9-10

BIBLICAL BASIS
John 15:13; 1 John 2:9-11; 3:14-19; 4:9-11,18-21

THE BIG IDEA
One of the marks of being a Christian is loving those around you.

PREPARATION
- A video camera and a blank videocassette
- A TV and a VCR

Create a three- to five-minute word-on-the-street video by interviewing a few students about their thoughts on family and friends. Ask the following questions:
- Who is it that is hard for you to love? Why?
- What is one quick and easy way to show love for another person?

Outline

WHAT'S LOVE GOT TO DO WITH IT?

The Big Idea
One of the marks of being a Christian is loving those around you.

INTRODUCTION

Show the video; then transition with: **Whether we like it or not—and whether they make it easy or not—we are called to love those around us. This is not an option; it's our calling.**

In John 15:13, we are called to love one another as Christ loves us.

BODY OF THE MESSAGE

Loving others is what we are called to do as Christians. In loving others, we show two very important things to the world.

I. Loving Others Shows That We Know God—1 John 3:14-19

A. "This then is how we know that we belong to the truth" (1 John 3:19).
 1. When we love others, we are showing that we know God and have a relationship with Him.
 2. God *is* love.
B. Read 1 John 2:9-11. If we choose not to love those around us, we are still in darkness.
 1. In refusing to love others, we continue to be blinded by the darkness.
 2. In refusing to love others, we remain focused on ourselves. When we focus only on ourselves, we cannot see others through God's eyes.
C. Read 1 John 3:17. Words count, but actions speak louder.
D. Read 1 John 4:9-11. God didn't just love us; He acted on His love for us. Recognizing someone's need isn't enough; unless we act lovingly to help fill that need, we are not showing Christian love.

II. Loving Others Shows That We Love God—1 John 4:19-21

A. God initiated love.

B. Our love for God is a response to His love for us (given and acted upon).

C. God's love is many things.

   1. Passionate—It was His love for us that sent Jesus to die for our sins.

   2. Unconditional—It is given no matter what we've done.

   3. Committed—It is unwavering and committed to action.

D. Read 1 John 4:20-21. You only love Jesus as much as you love the person you love the least.

   1. We are called to love each other to the same extent that God loves us.

   2. We need to choose to love those around us because of the incredible love that God has given us.

CHALLENGE/ACTION STEPS

1. Read 1 John 4:18. True love moves beyond fear.
   - Fear of rejection
   - Fear of getting uncomfortable
   - Fear of what others might think or say

2. Take the three-on-three challenge.
   - Think of the names of three people you know.
   - Think of three acts of love you can do for each person.

WHAT'S LOVE GOT TO DO WITH IT?

1. Who is it that is hard for you to love? Why?

2. What is one quick and easy way to show love for another person?

3. List the names of the people you selected for the three-on-three challenge and the three things you can do for each person to show God's love.

Overview

MAKING A KINGDOM IMPACT

TOPIC
Making an impact for Christ

DESCRIPTION
No matter who we are, God has called each of us to make a difference. For most of us, when we think of that calling, we tend to think about the big things we can do for God. The refreshing truth is that what God is looking for are the small acts of obedience that can change a single life. This message explodes the myth that making a Kingdom impact is about changing the world single-handedly and focuses attention on daily differences.

KEY VERSE
"The King will reply, 'I tell you the truth, whatever you did for one of the least of these brothers of mine, you did for me.'" Matthew 25:40

BIBLICAL BASIS
Ezekiel 22:30; Matthew 25:31-46

THE BIG IDEA
God is looking for people who will do "whatever" to make a Kingdom impact.

PREPARATION
- 3x5-inch index cards
- Pens or pencils

Think about a time when you were obedient to do "whatever" to minister to someone else. You could use a student's story instead—but get permission first! The illustration should focus on the impact that small obedient acts have on the Kingdom.

Outline

MAKING A KINGDOM IMPACT

The Big Idea
God is looking for people who will do "whatever" to make a Kingdom impact.

INTRODUCTION

Consider This
The year was 1989 and Nicolae Ceausescu was ruling the country of Romania. Out on the front steps of a sixteenth-century church 15 children sang hymns and prayed for freedom in Trimisorra, Romania. They were protesting the evil leadership of Nicolae Ceausescu and the lack of freedom in their beautiful country. Nicolae Ceausescu publicly announced when he took over power that "within 25 years, I will wipe away Christmas and Easter from the memories of the Romanian people."

As they sang and prayed, others watched and still others sat inside the church to support and pray for them. Ceausescu's secret police also stood by in silence until they received the word they were waiting for—then they raised their AK-47s and murdered every child in the group. Over the next few weeks, thousands of Romanian people came to that same square, with candles lit, singing hymns, all in remembrance of those 15 children. Within weeks, Ceausescu's regime was overthrown. Ironically, he and his wife were both executed on national television on Christmas day. The country was free—all because 15 children chose to take a stand for what they believed in.

We live in a scary time in our world and yet God continues to use young people to start revivals and crush oppression. God is using youth to make a difference in the world. You can radically change your world, if you choose to.

In Ezekiel 22:30, God was looking for people who would stand up and make an impact for His kingdom. Will you heed His call to stand in the gap?

BODY OF THE MESSAGE

Making an impact for the Kingdom means showing God's mercy every day.

I. Helping Those in Need—Matthew 25:31-46

A. Read Matthew 25:34-39. We are to be sensitive to the needs of others.

 1. Compassion is seeing the needs of others as we look at others through the eyes of Christ.

 2. It's easy to use excuses for not reaching out ("I'm too busy." "Someone else can do it better." "I'm only one person, so what can I do?").

 3. Jesus longs for us to open our eyes and see the needs that He sees.

 4. The key to having compassion is having your heart broken. Is your heart broken with the things that break the heart of God?

> **Consider This**
>
> When she received the Nobel Peace Prize in 1979, Mother Teresa was asked by an interviewer, "Why is it that you've committed your life to the sick and dying in the streets of Calcutta?" Her reply was staggering. "I haven't committed my life to the sick and dying of Calcutta. I've committed my life to Jesus, and it just so happens that I see His face on the sick and dying of Calcutta."

B. Read Matthew 25:40. We are to look for Jesus in the faces of those in need.

 1. When you serve and minister to those around you, you're serving and ministering to Jesus Himself.

 2. When we tangibly reach out to minister to those in need, we truly are ministering and showing love to Jesus Himself.

 3. Have you seen the face of Jesus lately?

II. Serving with What You Have—Matthew 25:40

A. Read Matthew 25:40. We are to serve with "whatever": whatever we have and whatever we can do.

 1. God is not necessarily looking for the talented but for the willing.

 a. God is *not* looking for someone to change the whole world single-handedly.

 b. God *is* looking for people who will serve in the small things!

 2. We all have more to give than we might think.

 3. Making a Kingdom difference means ordinary people doing ordinary things through the power of an extraordinary God.

> **Consider This**
> Share your personal (or a student's) illustration about a time when you were obedient to do the "whatever" (Matthew 25:40) to minister to someone.

CHALLENGE/ACTION STEPS

1. Take the next few moments in silent prayer; then write down on an index card what you need to do this week because of what you've learned during this message. Here are some ideas:
   - Write the name of someone you need to serve and how you might serve him or her.
   - Write an area in your life that you need to confess and turn over to God.
   - Write a ministry you feel called to serve.
2. Whatever you've written down, don't let those things be forgotten—take action on them this week.

MAKING A KINGDOM IMPACT

1. Read Matthew 25:31-46. In the left column list the similarities between the sheep and the goats. In the right column list the differences.

Similarities	Differences

2. In what ways are we like the sheep?

3. In what ways are we like the goats?

4. What can you do to serve God with who you are and what you have?

5. What keeps us from being sensitive to the needs of those around us?

6. What do you think breaks God's heart?

7. What can you do to be more sensitive, letting God break your heart for others?

8. Read Philippians 4:13. If you could serve Jesus in any way, what would you do? What keeps you from doing it?

Overview

DON'T JUST DO SOMETHING—STAND THERE!

TOPIC
Spending quality time with God

DESCRIPTION
We can be so busy about the work of God, that we miss just being with God. Busyness is something that plagues us all as Christians. This message examines the life of two sisters, Mary and Martha, both of whom loved Jesus, but who had very different expectations and experiences in His presence.

KEY VERSE
"She had a sister called Mary, who sat at the Lord's feet listening to what he said." Luke 10:39

BIBLICAL BASIS
Psalm 46:10; Luke 10:39-42; John 11:28-34; 12:1-3

THE BIG IDEA
What we do *with* Christ is so much more important than what we do *for* Him.

PREPARATION
Think of a time when the busyness of your life got in the way of what was really important—time with God.

Outline

DON'T JUST DO SOMETHING—STAND THERE!

> **The Big Idea**
> What we do *with* Christ is so much more important than what we do *for* Him.

INTRODUCTION

God teaches us eternal lessons in the midst of everyday life.

> **Consider This**
> Share your personal illustration and how your busyness kept you from fellowship with God.

We can be so busy about the work of God, that we can miss being with God. Every day we make a choice to either sit at His feet or be busy about our agenda.

BODY OF THE MESSAGE

Spending time with God is more important than being busy for Him.

I. A Devoted Servant—Luke 10:39

Mary was completely devoted to Jesus.
1. Read John 11:28-34. Mary ran to meet Jesus outside of the village.
2. Read John 12:1-3. Mary anointed Jesus' feet with expensive perfume, a sign that nothing was too good for her Master.
3. Read Luke 10:39. Mary sat at the Lord's feet, reverently drinking in His every word.

II. A Busy Servant—Luke 10:40

Martha thought more of the dinner in Jesus' honor than spending time with Jesus Himself.
1. "But Martha was distracted by all the preparations that had to be made." Luke 10:40
   a. Martha was so worried about the details that she didn't see the bigger picture.

b. Martha was resentful of Mary's apparent lack of concern for all that had to be done.

2. Sometimes we are too focused on our own agenda and don't see what God's plan is.
   a. We can be so busy doing things for God, that we can miss being with God.
   b. The Pharisees had good intentions, but they were so consumed with the rules and regulations of Scripture and tradition that they forgot about actually having a relationship with God.

3. Read Luke 10:41. What we do *with* Christ is so much more important than what we do *for* Him.

Consider This

In Luke 10, Jesus' answer to Martha was incredibly tender and affection-ate, "Martha, Martha . . . you are worried and upset about many things" (v. 41). He wanted her affection, not her activity.

"Only one thing is needed" (v. 42). At that moment, only one thing really mattered—being with Him. "Mary has chosen" (v. 42). Fellowship and communing with God are an indication of our priorities: a choice to stop, be still and seek Him.

CHALLENGE/ACTION STEPS

Few things are as damaging to the Christian life as working for Christ without tak-ing the time to commune with Him.

1. It all comes down to choice. Are we choosing what we *think* we need to do for Jesus' sake?
2. Choose to live Psalm 46:10: "Be still, and know that I am God."
3. Busyness can cover up a fear of stillness, a fear of silence. We can be scared to find that our spiritual life is hollow, shallow or empty. But Jesus knows and He calls us to be still so that He can bring depth and substance to our lives. Here are a few things to consider this week:
   - Stop—Slow or stop the activity. Choose to slow down and set some time aside to be still.
   - Still—Be still in attention. Find a place to be alone and sit before Jesus, listening to His voice and His Word. Allow Him to speak to your heart.
   - Seek—Seek Him in authenticity. Open your heart to Him in honest prayer, worship and communion with Him.

PRAYER TIME

Allow students to have a few minutes alone in silence to commune with God. Begin or end the time of silence by sharing the following quote:

Consider This

Dear Savior at whose feet I now sit,

When you knock on the door to my heart, what is it you're looking for? What is it you want? Is it not to come in to dine with me? Is it not for fellowship?

And yet, so often, where do you find me? At your feet? No. In the kitchen. How many times have I become distracted and left you there . . . sitting . . . waiting . . . longing?

What is so important about my kitchenful of preparations that draws me away from you? How can they seem so trivial now and yet so urgent when I'm caught up in them?

Forgive me for being so much distracted by my preparations and so little attracted by your presence. For being so diligent in my duties and so negligent in my devotion. For being so quick to my feet and so slow to yours.

Help me to understand that it is an intimate moment you seek from me, not an elaborate meal.[1]

Note

1. Ken Gire, *Intense Moments with the Savior* (Grand Rapids, MI: Zondervan Publishing House, 1994), p. 69.

DON'T JUST DO SOMETHING—STAND THERE!

1. Do you identify more with Mary or Martha?

2. What are you busy with that might interfere with your time with God?

4. What choices do you need to make in order to experience the intimacy with God that He wants to have with you?

5. How can others help keep you accountable in those choices?

Overview

LIVING INSIDE OUT

TOPIC
Religion versus relationship

DESCRIPTION
God hates religion. Religion is our attempt to look good enough for God. What God desires is a relationship, not religion. He doesn't want our outer religiousness and our attempts to look good in His sight. What He desires is that we come to Him in surrender, allowing Him to transform us from the inside out. This message encourages students to move away from legalism and religion toward a completely surrendered and transformed life in relationship with almighty God.

KEY VERSE
"As he neared Damascus on his journey, suddenly a light from heaven flashed around him. He fell to the ground and heard a voice say to him, 'Saul, Saul, why do you persecute me?'

" 'Who are you, Lord?' Saul asked.

" 'I am Jesus, whom you are persecuting,' he replied. 'Now get up and go into the city, and you will be told what you must do.' " Acts 9:3-6

BIBLICAL BASIS
Matthew 5:20; John 3:16-17; Acts 9:1-14; 28:30-31; Romans 3:21-26; 12:3; Ephesians 2:4-5,8-9

THE BIG IDEA
Christianity isn't about religion; it's about relationship.

PREPARATION
- The items necessary to present a slide show or PowerPoint presentation
- Pictures of yourself as a child (if you can, find pictures that depict you pretending to be something: athlete, astronaut, cowboy/cowgirl, prince/princess, etc.)

Have your pictures made into slides or scan them into a PowerPoint program.

Outline

LIVING INSIDE OUT

> **The Big Idea**
> Christianity isn't about religion; it's about relationship.

INTRODUCTION

Things aren't always as they appear.

> **Object Lesson**
> As you show your childhood pictures, make sure that you have fun at your own expense. Students will connect with you as they see photographs of you as a child.

Being a Christian is more than being good enough or looking the part on the outside; we have to be changed on the inside. Simply looking the part or going through the motions isn't what God wants from us, and if that's our view of what being a Christian looks like, we'll always fall short of God's plan.

Religion focuses on the outside, making sure that you look the part. Relationship develops the inside, making sure that you are what you say you are. "For all have sinned and fall short of the glory of God, and are justified freely by his grace through the redemption that came by Christ Jesus" (Romans 3:23-24).

BODY OF THE MESSAGE

A guy named Saul encountered God—not religion—and was changed forever. There are two life-changing truths you can bank your soul on.

I. Being a Christian Is Life Transforming—Acts 9:1-3

A. Paul tried being good enough and found that it didn't matter.
  1. The Pharisees thought they were flawless and blameless in keeping the law. Read Matthew 5:20. Righteousness is more than following the rules.
  2. Paul was a live-and-die-by-the-rules guy before he met Jesus. Read Acts 9:13-14. He worked under the complete authority of the chief priests.
B. Paul encountered the living God and was changed forever.
  1. Read Ephesians 2:8-9. Having a relationship with God means being changed from the inside out, not the outside in.
    a. "Inside out" means approaching God, asking Him to change us and

help us follow His direction for our lives.

    b. "Outside in" means doing all the right things and trying to look good in God's eyes.

  2. Being a Christian transforms your life (your values, attitudes and actions). Read Acts 28:30-31—Paul's value, attitudes and actions were transformed.

II. Being a Christian Is About Surrender—Acts 9:3-9

A. Read Acts 9:3-4. Saul was a very powerful man, yet he was brought to his knees by the very sight of Jesus.

B. Read Romans 12:3. We are called to be humble before God and man.

  1. Christianity doesn't call out, "Look at what an asset I am to Christianity!"

  2. Christianity quietly says, "God, there is nothing in me that is worthy of You, but I really need You, Lord. I surrender to You. You alone are my hope."

C. Read Ephesians 2:4-5. We have nothing to offer God that He needs. He desires our love and offered Christ as a sacrifice to bring us back to Him.

  1. Read Romans 3:21-26. God initiated our reconciliation to Him.

  2. Read John 3:16-17. All we have to do is surrender to Christ.

CHALLENGE/ACTION STEPS

  1. Are you trying to conform to what you think a Christian is supposed to be?

  2. If you're too busy, what will it take for God to get your attention?

  3. It's when we've seen our need for Christ and surrendered to Him that we can fully seek Him. Are you ready to surrender?

LIVING INSIDE OUT

1. What do you think about the statement "Christianity isn't about religion; it's about relationship"?

2. What is the true difference between religion and relationship?

3. What does God really desire in a relationship with us?

4. Why is it so difficult to totally surrender to God?

5. What do you need to do this week to seek God in relationship, rather than in religion?

Overview

FORGET ME, FORGET ME NOT

TOPIC
Remembering God

DESCRIPTION
We can play the role of the forgetful follower of Jesus. When times are great, we move through life with little more than a brief thought of God. Yet when times are difficult, we approach God in earnest. God's desire is that we live *every* moment of our lives in constant remembrance of who He is and what He has done. This message explores ways in which we can practically remember God daily.

KEY VERSE
"Only be careful, and watch yourselves closely so that you do not forget the things your eyes have seen or let them slip from your heart as long as you live. Teach them to your children and to their children after them." Deuteronomy 4:9

BIBLICAL BASIS
Deuteronomy 4:9-14; 8:10-20; 1 Samuel 15:22-23; Psalm 105:1-7; 1 Corinthians 11:24-25

THE BIG IDEA
God is calling His people to honor Him by remembering who He is and what He has done for them.

PREPARATION
- Paper
- Pens or pencils

Prepare a personal illustration about a time when things were going well and you took God for granted, only to realize later how much you really need Him all the time.

Outline

FORGET ME, FORGET ME NOT

> **The Big Idea**
> God is calling His people to honor Him by remembering who He is and what He has done for them.

INTRODUCTION

Share your personal illustration; then explain how we are sometimes like the Israelites, taking God for granted, calling on Him only when we're desperate.

As Christians we are called to remember what God has done for us all the time.

BODY OF THE MESSAGE

I. A Portrait of Forgetfulness—Deuteronomy 8:10-18

It's easy to become forgetful when things are going well.
A. Read Deuteronomy 8:10-13. Complacence: We forget God when we're comfortable.
B. Read Deuteronomy 8:14. Conceit: We forget God when we're proud and full of ourselves.
C. Read Deuteronomy 8:17-18. Competence: We forget God when we think we don't need Him (i.e., we can do it all on our own).

II. A Call to Remember—Deuteronomy 4:9-14

A. God's desire is that we not forget who He is and what He has done.
B. How do we remember and honor God?
   1. Read Deuteronomy 4:9 and Psalm 105:1-7. We tell others about Him.
   2. We should share with others what God is doing in our lives.
   3. We should share with others God's desire to change their lives. When we share what God is doing, we bring Him into the present and honor Him as the living and active God.

   4. Read 1 Corinthians 11:24-25. We participate in Communion to remember that Jesus, God's own Son, died for us to be reconciled to Him.
C. Read Deuteronomy 8:18-20 and 1 Samuel 15:22-23. We seek to be obedient to God's will.
   1. When we choose to obey God, we honor Him as God.
   2. What delights the heart of God is
      • not our religiousness (i.e., looking good on the outside) but
      • our inward devotion of obedience and
      • remembering that He is in charge, not us.

CHALLENGE/ACTION STEPS

   1. God is calling each of us to remember Him and what He's done and is doing in our lives. Will we continue to have selective memory, remembering God only when we have a crisis?
   2. Take a few moments to write a letter to God. Praise Him for who He is. Thank Him for what He has been doing in your life lately.

Suggestion
Collect the students' letters and post them on a wall in the meeting area as a reminder to everyone of who God is and what He has been doing in the lives of your students.

FORGET ME, FORGET ME NOT

1. Why is it so easy to forget about God?

2. What benefits are there in remembering God's presence in our lives?

3. What choices do we need to make daily to remember God?

4. What is something that God has been doing in your life lately?

5. What can you do to remember God's presence in that situation?

Overview

BEING A GOD SEEKER—
A MESSAGE FOR YOUNG MEN

TOPIC
Seeking God, brokenness, repentance and commitment

DESCRIPTION
This message focuses on the characteristics and attributes of what God is searching for in biblical manhood, as opposed to what today's world says a man should be.

> **Note**
> As written, this message is designed for male students; however, it's concepts are transferable to women as well.

KEY VERSE
"Josiah was eight years old when he became king, and he reigned in Jerusalem thirty-one years. He did what was right in the eyes of the LORD and walked in the ways of his father David, not turning aside to the right or the left. In the eighth year of his reign, while he was still young, he began to seek the God of his father David." 2 Chronicles 34:1-3

BIBLICAL BASIS
Deuteronomy 30:15,17-20; 2 Chronicles 34:1-3,18-21,26-34; Psalms 24:1-6; 51:17; Jeremiah 29:11-14; Ezekiel 22:30

THE BIG IDEA
God is looking for men who will seek after Him.

PREPARATION
- The *Braveheart* video (Paramount Pictures, 1995)
- The *Titanic* video (20th Century Fox, 1997)
- A TV and a VCR

Cue each video to the appropriate scene. For *Braveheart,* use the freedom speech that William Wallace (played by Mel Gibson) gives to the troops just before going into battle together. This scene comes approximately one hour and 17 minutes into the film. Be sure to start *after* the "bolts of lightning" line. For *Titanic,* use the bow-of-the-ship scene in which Jack Dawson (played by Leonardo DiCaprio) shows a softer side of being a true man.

Outline

BEING A GOD SEEKER—
A MESSAGE FOR YOUNG MEN

> **The Big Idea**
> God is looking for men who will seek after Him.

INTRODUCTION

Show both video clips exemplifying the ways in which Hollywood and American culture define what a true man is. Explain: **Today's society holds up images of what it means to be a man. Let's take a look at the type of man God is looking for.**

According to Ezekiel 22:30, God is looking. What will He find?

BODY OF THE MESSAGE

As we study the story of King Josiah, we encounter a man God can use.

I. A Man Seeks After God—2 Chronicles 34:1-3

A. Josiah made tough decisions, starting at a very young age.
   1. Read 2 Chronicles 34:1. He was only eight years old when he began his reign.
   2. Read 2 Chronicles 34:3. At age 20, he began a huge purging of all false images, altars and idols.

B. From the beginning, Josiah sought to do the right thing.
   1. "He did what was right in the eyes of the LORD and walked in the ways of his father David" (2 Chronicles 34:2).
   2. At age 16, he "began to seek the God of his father David" (2 Chronicles 34:3).

C. God is looking for men who will seek after Him as Josiah did.
   1. Seeking after God involves self-sacrifice and tough decisions. We seek Him for decisions, wisdom, blessing, etc., but do we truly seek *Him*? We seek after His blessings (from His hands), but do we seek to know Him (seek His face)?

2. God promises to be found if we seek Him "with all our heart" (Jeremiah 29:11-14).

  a. We need to seek after God with reckless abandon, seeking His face in earnest, no matter where He leads us.

  b. God isn't looking for perfect people; He wants people, imperfections and all, who will be open, available and passionately seeking Him.

II. A Man Is Broken Before God—2 Chronicles 34:18-21

A. Read Psalm 51:17. God desires that we are broken over sin. Brokenness is often seen as weakness in today's world, but God views brokenness differently.

  1. We are broken when we see God for who He really is and see ourselves as we really are: sinners.

  2. Only when we are broken can God use us.

  3. Only when we are broken does our pride move aside.

  4. Only when we are broken do we really understand the love of God and see Christ as the answer for this world and for ourselves. If we don't see the problem, we won't search for the answer.

B. When we seek God, He will reveal Himself to us.

  1. Read 2 Chronicles 34:14-21. Josiah desperately sought the Lord's will regarding the Book of the Law.

    a. God commanded His people to "keep his commands, decrees and laws" (Deuteronomy 30:15).

    b. Read Deuteronomy 30:17-18. The Lord warned of what would happen if the people ignored His commands.

  2. Read 2 Chronicles 34:19. Josiah was broken to find that the Lord's Word had not been obeyed. He was broken both for the nation and his own personal sin.

III. A Man Confesses Before God—2 Chronicles 34:26-28

A. Josiah in his brokenness sent Hilkiah to inquire of God, and God heard and replied through Huldah.

  1. Josiah confessed his sin and the sin of the nation. As he humbled himself before the Lord, God was glorified and answered.

    • "Because your heart was responsive . . . and you humbled yourself before me and tore your robes and wept in my presence, I have heard you, declares the LORD" (2 Chronicles 34:27).

  2. God is looking for men who will not only be broken over sin but who will also deal with it head-on and repent in brokenness.

a. Repentance is not a subject we like to talk about in our society.

b. Conviction without change is just wasted emotion.

IV. A Man Is Renewed By God—2 Chronicles 34:29-34

A. Josiah's conviction and brokenness moved him into action.

1. Read 2 Chronicles 34:31. Josiah committed himself to making things right with God without counting the personal cost and in spite of what others might think.

2. Read 2 Chronicles 34:32. Josiah's actions spread to all the people.

3. Read 2 Chronicles 34:33. Josiah acted on his commitment to God.

B. If you want to have a passionate and intimate relationship with Jesus Christ, then obedience to His voice is key.

1. Have you heard His voice lately?

a. We should leave bad attitudes and habits behind.

b. We should make a commitment to change some things at home (e.g., heal relationships, seek forgiveness).

c. We should do business with God before we leave this meeting.

2. Are you the type of man God is seeking? When He searches for faithful, broken and obedient men, will He find you?

CHALLENGE/ACTION STEPS

1. Commit yourself privately.
   - Count the cost.
   - Search your heart and ask, *Am I seeking, broken, confessing and repentant?*
2. Commit yourself personally.
   - Seek after God passionately and intimately.
   - Seek to obey His Word and His voice.
3. Commit yourself publicly.
   - Make a choice to make the changes you need to.
   - Make a choice to get rid of the stuff in your life that entangles you.

COMMITMENT TIME

Take a few moments at the close of the message to give students the time and opportunity to deal with God in whatever way He is speaking to them. Students may need to confess sin. They may want to worship God and say "God, I want to seek you!" Have a time of worship and personal response for students.

BEING A GOD SEEKER—
A MESSAGE FOR YOUNG MEN

1. What action do you need to take because of what God said to you today?

2. Where do you want to make an impact?

3. Read Psalm 24:1-6 as a group. What does your youth group need to do or change to be the generation that seeks the face of God?

4. Spend some time in prayer for your group and for each other that you'd be the generation that seeks the face of God and impacts your church, community, schools and families for Jesus Christ.

Overview

GETTING A HEART CHECKUP

TOPIC
Examining the state of your heart

DESCRIPTION
God desires to speak to each of us through His Word, but the state of our heart has much to do with our ability to hear Him. In this message, we will examine the parable of the soils to gain insight into the state of our hearts. The goal in the end is to have an open and hungry heart for the voice of God in our lives.

KEY VERSE
"Others, like seed sown on good soil, hear the word, accept it, and produce a crop—thirty, sixty or even a hundred times what was sown." Mark 4:20

BIBLICAL BASIS
Matthew 6:27; Mark 4:1-20

THE BIG IDEA
God wants to speak to you. Will you have the ears and heart to listen?

PREPARATION
• Four pieces of poster board and a felt-tip pen
• A bucket of seeds

Use the poster board and marker to create four signs: "Good Soil," "Rocky Soil," "Thorny Soil" and "Soil Along the Path."

Outline

GETTING A HEART CHECKUP

The Big Idea
God wants to speak to you. Will you have the ears and heart to listen?

INTRODUCTION

Spontaneous Melodrama
Using the actual text of Mark 4:1-20 as your script, recruit five volunteers to improvise and interpret the passage for the audience. Give the soil signs to four of the volunteers and the bucket of seeds to the fifth volunteer. Read through the parable, stopping frequently to allow the actors to provide their creative interpretations of the parable. The more creative and outgoing your volunteers, the better.

What's the state of your heart today? If God were to speak to you, would you hear Him?

BODY OF THE MESSAGE

Just as the four soils had different responses to the seed, so our hearts can have four different responses to the seed of God's Word.

I. Hardened Soil—Mark 4:3-15

A. When our hearts are hardened, we are prevented from hearing God's Word.

B. We need to break down the walls we've built around our hearts.
   1. The walls go up because we've been hurt by others.
   2. The walls allow us to feel safe—if no one can get through, we can't be hurt.
   3. We don't let anyone through our walled hearts—including God.

C. Having a hardened heart makes us cynical, critical and guarded.

II. Shallow Soil—Mark 4:5-6,16-17

A. When our hearts have shallow soil, the seeds of God's Word can be planted, but they won't become deeply rooted and change our lives.

1. Shallow soil causes us to consider the "God thing" but not take any steps to change how we live.
2. Shallow soil causes us to be interested in Christianity on the surface, but it doesn't give us the desire to dig deeper into God's will for our lives. Maybe you're trying to change yourself from the outside in.
B. When our hearts have shallow soil, we don't have God to hang onto in tough times.

III. Distracted Soil—Mark 4:7,18-19

A. When our hearts are distracted, God's voice gets drowned out in the sea of other noise: worries and cares, lure of wealth or desire for other things. When we're distracted, we get sidetracked by things that pull the focus off God.
B. When our hearts are distracted, it's time to stop, listen and regain our focus. Sometimes worries are what distract us most.
1. "Who of you by worrying can add a single hour to his life?" (Matthew 6:27).
2. We need to put our worries in the right perspective, trusting God with all that concerns us.

IV. Hungry Soil—Mark 4:8,20

A. A hungry heart hears the voice of God and accepts it. When we're hungry for God's Word, His seeds grow within us.
B. A hungry heart is ready for God to work.
1. God wants us to be open and willing to hear His voice.
2. God wants us to seek His voice.
3. God wants us to be willing to act on what He tells us.

CHALLENGE/ACTION STEPS
1. Seed It—If your heart is *hard*, open it up to God; allow the seed to take hold in your life.
2. Feed It—If your heart is *shallow*, let Him change you; seek to grow in your love relationship with God.
3. Weed It—If your heart is *distracted*, remove the weeds and distractions that are pulling you away from the loving God, choking your love relationship with Him.

GETTING A HEART CHECKUP

1. Has God been speaking to you lately? What has He been saying?

2. What has been your reaction to His voice in your life?

3. What makes it difficult to hear God's voice in your life?

4. Which soil is most like your heart? Why?

5. Which of the action steps do you need to take? What will you do about it this week?

Overview

UNCLOGGING YOUR ARTERIES— CLEANING YOUR HEART

TOPIC
Dealing with sin and your heart

DESCRIPTION
Scripture reminds us that "all have sinned and fall short of the glory of God" (Romans 3:23). There is not a person alive that falls outside of that statement. At some point or another, we all have to deal with the sin in our lives. At that moment, we have a choice. Do we cover over our sin by trying to look good on the outside, ignoring our inner sinfulness? Or do we freely come to Christ, broken and desiring mercy and forgiveness? This message examines the type of repentant heart that pleases and brings glory to God.

KEY VERSE
"Have mercy on me, O God, according to your unfailing love; according to your great compassion blot out my transgressions. Wash away all my iniquity and cleanse me from my sin." Psalm 51:1-2

BIBLICAL BASIS
Psalm 51:1-12,17; Romans 3:23; 1 John 1:9; 5:3

THE BIG IDEA
God is in the business of changing hard hearts to soft ones.

PREPARATION
- Latex gloves
- A disposable pie tin
- A large can of dog food
- Chocolate frosting
- A serving plate
- A knife, a serving spatula and a fork

Prepare a pie: Wearing latex gloves, fill the pie tin with the dog food. Allow pie to set for an hour or so in the refrigerator; then cover it with chocolate frosting.

Outline

UNCLOGGING YOUR ARTERIES— CLEANING YOUR HEART

> **The Big Idea**
> God is in the business of changing hard hearts to soft ones.

INTRODUCTION

What's on the inside of something isn't always apparent by looking at the outside.

> **Object Lesson**
> Explain that you've been studying cooking during your time off and wanted to show off your newfound talent by making this chocolate pie, and you're wondering if anyone would like to try some of your creation. Dip your finger (VERY carefully) into the chocolate and lick off the frosting. Invite a student up for a sampling. Have the student cut the pie and serve a piece. The aroma and consistency will be an immediate giveaway as to the contents of your "chocolate pie." Follow up by explaining: **Our lives often resemble this pie. We sure look good on the outside, but after you get past the thin layer of our exterior . . . yuck! Some of us come here and look good on the outside, but what about the inside? God wants to clean your heart. He knows what's there and loves you just the same!**

Psalm 51:1-12 describes God's plan for unclogging the arteries of our heart!

BODY OF THE MESSAGE

A hard heart is closed to God and the things He wants to give us. A soft heart is open to what God desires and wants to use in our lives. There are four things we can do to have S-O-F-T hearts.

I. S—Search Your Heart—Psalm 51:1-3

    A. If we were to do an EKG of your thoughts, desires, actions, faith, words and behavior, what would the EKG reveal?

    B. As you look at your heart, what do you see?

II. O—Openly Confess from Your Heart—Psalm 51:4-7

A. Confessing means bringing our sin before Him (v. 4), not hiding our sin, but exposing it for what it really is.

B. Do we try and hide our sin? Are we broken over our sin?

C. Read Psalm 51:17. God doesn't despise a broken, or contrite, heart. He delights in it, because He can work within it!

D. Jesus knows your sin. Don't try to hide it—bring it to Him!

III. F—Freshly Seek After God with All Your Heart—Psalm 51:8-10

A. The great news of the gospel is that no matter what you've done or where you've been, Jesus knows and can forgive.

   1. Read 1 John 1:9. There is nothing God cannot or will not forgive.

   2. Are we willing to confess and bring our sin to Him?

B. Most of us have recycling trash cans. Recycling is about taking something that seems useless and making it useful again. That's what God does with our lives!

C. Read Psalm 51:10. God can give us new hearts; all we have to do is ask.

IV. T—Tune In to God's Voice with an Obedient Heart— Psalm 51:11-12

A. David is saying, "Don't make me unusable. I want to be used!"

B. As we seek after God, we need to be willing to obey Him (because we love Him and as a response for all that He has done).

   1. We need to obey because we love Him. In fact, our obedience shows that we love God (see 1 John 5:3).

   2. We need to love Him, trusting that He has our best in mind.

CHALLENGE/ACTION STEPS

Take the time right now to do some business with God.

   1. **Examine** your heart (evaluate what you see, say and seek after).

   2. **Express** to God what you find there (confess your sin, bringing it to Him).

   3. **Engage** a plan to guard your heart (take action on those sins by repenting).

   4. **Enlist** the help of others (find someone who can hold you accountable).

UNCLOGGING YOUR ARTERIES— CLEANING YOUR HEART

1. How can our lives be like the pie filled with dog food?

2. What is the good news of 1 John 1:9? How does it apply to each of our lives?

3. What commitment did you make today? How do you want your life to be different after what you've heard?

4. What can we do as a group to help keep you accountable for your commitment?

5. Close your discussion time by praying for the needs and commitments of each person in your group.

SMALL GROUP BIBLE STUDY OUTLINES— A STUDY OF JAMES

*　*　*
*

Overview

Boy, It's Getting Hot in Here!
(James 1:2-4,12)

TOPIC
Surviving trials

DESCRIPTION
When it comes to trials, it's not a matter of *if* but *when* we will encounter them in our lives. The key to getting through them is to avoid asking *why* and begin asking *what. What are You producing in my life, God?* It is in the midst of trials that God does some of His most amazing work. This lesson focuses on the benefits of going through trials, offering hope and strength in the midst of the storms.

KEY VERSE
"Consider it pure joy, my brothers, whenever you face trials of many kinds, because you know that the testing of your faith develops perseverance. Perseverance must finish its work so that you may be mature and complete, not lacking anything." James 1:2-4

BIBLICAL BASIS
Job 42:1-6; Psalm 13; 2 Corinthians 1:3-5; James 1:2-4,12

THE BIG IDEA
God has a purpose for our trials—to make us holy.

SESSION AIMS
During this session you will guide students to do the following:
- Examine the issues and benefits of trials in their lives
- Discover how God uses trials to bring about holiness and His likeness
- Implement a change of attitude, mind, will and heart toward the trials they face

PREPARATION

In the week prior to this lesson, look in the news for stories of people going through tough times and trials. Read the newspaper, watch newscasts on television and explore the Internet. The more current the situation, the better. The more unresolved the situation, the better. The goal is to bring a current trial, or struggle, into the group as a current case study. If you find a written story, be sure to make enough copies for everyone in your group.

OUTLINE

BOY, IT'S GETTING HOT IN HERE!
(JAMES 1:2-4,12)

The Big Idea
God has a purpose for our trials—to make us holy.

INTRODUCTION

Read through the news story you selected; then briefly discuss the nature of the problem and how the people involved might be feeling, thinking and reacting.

IN THE WORD

We all go through tough times. Instead of asking why we have to go through them, we should be asking God what He's producing through them in our lives.

Discussion
- What was one trial that you have gone through in the past month?
- What are some words that come to mind when you think about that trial?
- What are some lessons you've learned about yourself and God from that particular trial?
- What are some benefits of going through tough times?

I. Trials Develop Maturity and Faith—James 1:2-4

A. God's plan for trials is to make us holy and more like Him.
   1. Trials put our faith to the test and help us develop perseverance.
      a. Perseverance comes from a commitment to God that is based on trust, not feelings or blessings.
      b. Perseverance's purpose is maturity and completeness. Trials strip away our good feelings of the easy Christian life and focus us on the truth and reality of following Jesus, even when it's tough.
   2. Trials strip away our good feelings of the easy Christian life and focus us on the truth of following Jesus, even when it's tough.

> **Discussion**
> - What comes to mind when you hear the statement "God's plan for trials is not to make us happy in life but to make us holy"?
> - How would you define the word "perseverance"?
> - James 1:4 tells us that when we persevere through trials, we won't lack anything. What does this mean?
> - What benefits do trials produce in Christians?

II. Trials Develop God-Centeredness—Psalm 13

A. God's plan for trials is to draw our attention away from ourselves and toward Him.

B. Were it not for trials, we could easily develop an attitude of self-sufficiency and think, *I don't need God—I can handle life without Him.*.

C. Trials force us to our knees in total dependence on God, crying out to Him, "I desperately need You, I have no other hope than You!"

> **Discussion**
> - When was the last time you felt like praying the first two verses of Psalm 13?
> - Which part of those verses can you most relate to right now? Why?
> - In Psalm 13:3, David cries out to God for help and insight. Think about your life right now; what are the cries of your heart? What do you need to hear from God?
> - Why could David pray Psalm 13:5-6 in the midst of his trial?
> - What can we learn from what David wrote in Psalm 13?

III. Trials Develop Compassion—2 Corinthians 1:3-5

A. God uses our trials to make us sensitive to others.

B. Our trials make us more compassionate, enabling us to extend God's grace and comfort to others.

C. Our trials give others hope and strength to reach out to God and keep persevering.

> **Discussion**
> - What are the two titles God is given in 2 Corinthians 1:3? What hope can they give to someone going through a tough time?
> - According to 2 Corinthians 1:4, what is one purpose of our trials?

- Have you ever been comforted by someone who had been through a trial similar to the one you were going through? How did it feel?
- Have you ever comforted someone else going through tough times because you understood what he or she was going through? How did that feel?
- What promise are we given in 2 Corinthians 1:5?

IV. Trials Develop a Deeper Intimacy with God—Job 42:1-6

A. Job went through some tremendous trials in his life.

B. The book of Job was *not* written to answer the question, Why do bad things happen to good people?

C. The book of Job describes the kind of faith that is developed in the midst of trials by a believer who is obedient to his God.

D. The book of Job was written to show how Job's trials produced an intimacy with God that he had never known before. "My ears had heard of you but now my eyes have seen you" (Job 42:5).

Discussion
- What essential truth is seen in Job 42:2?
- How does God's sovereignty impact our attitude in the midst of trials?
- How can trials draw us into deeper intimacy with God?

CHALLENGE/ACTION STEPS

We can either run away from our trials or embrace them as valuable lessons from God. Our trials are meant to make us more like Him.

Illustration
The refining of gold is a very interesting process. The substance is heated in a crucible until the impurities rise to the top. Then the impurities are wiped off the top of the heated mixture and the heat is turned up again. The process continues over and over again until the refiner's reflection can be seen perfectly on the surface of the liquid. As long as the refiner can't see his likeness clearly, there are still impurities that need to be brought out and wiped off.

There are four decisions we need to make during trials.

1. We must choose to have an attitude that is joyful (see James 1:2).
2. We must choose to have a mind that is understanding, believing that God is refining us to be a reflection of Him.
3. We must choose to have a will that is submissive to what God wants to do in our lives, allowing Him to continue bringing out our impurities in order to make us more like Him.
4. We must choose to have a trusting heart and be willing to allow God to refine and mold us for His purposes.

Discussion

- How is the refining process just like the trials we go through?
- What hope does the illustration about refining gold give you?
- Our response to trial is completely up to us. How will you respond?
- What is the final promise God gives in James 1:12? What does that promise mean to you?
- What is one thing that God has spoken to you about through this lesson? What will you do about it this week?

Overview

The Devil Made Me Do It!
(James 1:13-15)

TOPIC
Dealing with temptation

DESCRIPTION
No one is immune to temptation, not even Christians. How is it that we are so easily lead away into sin? This lesson explores what God's Word has to say about where temptation comes from, how it happens and what can ultimately be done to battle it.

KEY VERSE
"But each one is tempted when, by his own evil desire, he is dragged away and enticed. Then, after desire is conceived, it gives birth to sin; and sin, when it is full grown, gives birth to death." James 1:14-15

BIBLICAL BASIS
Genesis 3:1-16; 2 Samuel 11:1-15; Psalms 51:1-7; 119:9-16; Isaiah 6:3; Malachi 3:6; John 10:10; 1 Corinthians 10:13; James 1:13-15; 1 Peter 1:13-16; 1 John 1:8—2:2

THE BIG IDEA
God has given us every weapon we need to battle temptation in our lives.

SESSION AIMS
During this session you will guide students to do the following:
- Examine the issue of temptation in their lives
- Discover the origin and process of temptation
- Implement a plan of action for combating the temptations they will face

PREPARATION
- Paper
- Pens or pencils
- Optional: A white board and dry-erase marker

Outline

THE DEVIL MADE ME DO IT!
(JAMES 1:13-15)

The Big Idea
God has given us every weapon we need to battle temptation in our lives.

INTRODUCTION

Distribute paper and pens or pencils and instruct students to write down at least five temptations they face. Allow a few minutes; then invite students to share their lists. After everyone has shared, list the top five temptations (on the white board, if you chose to use it). Be sure to allow students to interact as you choose the top five, asking questions and stating their cases for their choices.

Discussion
- Which of our top five temptations were easy to agree upon?
- Which were more difficult to agree upon?
- What makes temptation so . . . tempting?
- How do people you know (or you yourself) fight these temptations?

IN THE WORD

One of the keys to battling temptation is recognizing where temptation comes from. God is holy and can never be unholy; therefore, He cannot be tempted by evil. God often tests, but never tempts. Why would God want us to fall into sin? He doesn't.

Discussion
- What does James 1:13-15 say about where temptation comes from?
- Why is it important for us to know that temptation doesn't come from God?
- What do Isaiah 6:3; Malachi 3:6; 1 Peter 1:13-16 and John 10:10 have to say about God's character and what He desires for our lives?

I. The Garden of Eden—Genesis 3:1-16

A. Even though we don't have to go looking for temptation, it's our responsibility to recognize it and turn from it.

B. Read Genesis 3:1-4. Eve stood there, listened to the serpent and was carried away by the temptation, letting her imagination run unchecked.

C. Read Genesis 3:5. Eve allowed herself to think about what it would be like to know the things God knows, lusting after something she wasn't supposed to have.

D. Read Genesis 3:6. Eve began to think about how enticing the fruit looked; her will began to weaken.

E. Read Genesis 3:6. Eve acted upon the thoughts she entertained, committing the act she had played out in her mind.

F. Read Genesis 3:7-16. In her greed, Eve convinced herself that only good could come from eating the forbidden fruit. She refused to consider the consequence of her actions.

II. David and Bathsheba—2 Samuel 11:1-15

A. Our decisions can place us in tempting situations, as David found out when he chose to send his army to fight without him.
   1. Read 2 Samuel 11:1-2. David was in the wrong place at the wrong time.
   2. Read 2 Samuel 11:3. Instead of turning from it, David allowed himself to become intrigued by the temptation of the woman bathing.
      a. He continued to look at the woman after he noticed her.
      b. He followed his lustful thought and made inquiries about the woman's identity.

B. Bowing to temptation drags us further into sin.
   1. Read 2 Samuel 11:4-5. Even though he knew she was married, David acted upon his temptation and the woman became pregnant.
   2. Read 2 Samuel 11:6-11. David still didn't think about how wrong he was; his only concern was that no one find out about his actions.
      a. Read 2 Samuel 11:10. He tried to cover up his sin.
      b. Read 2 Samuel 11:14-15. He compounded his wrongdoing by ordering an innocent man killed so that no one would find out.

Discussion
- At what point do you think Eve went wrong? Why?
- At what point do you think David went wrong? Why?
- What do you think was going through their minds in the midst of their temptations?
- At what point does temptation become a sin?

III. The Truth About Temptation—James 1:13-15

A. Read James 1:14. You *will* be tempted.

B. We are in trouble when we entertain our desires.

   1. When we entertain our desires, the desires become actions.

   2. When our desire "gives birth to sin," sin "gives birth to death" (James 1:15).

Discussion

- What do 1 Corinthians 10:13; Psalms 51:1-7; 119:9-16 and 1 John 1:8—2:2 tell us about how to avoid and survive temptation?

- If you were to design a guide for fellow students—a Top 10 Tips for Taking on Temptation—what would be your top 10 tips? (Suggestion: If you have a white board, use it to write responses, or take notes and type up a list to give the students at the next meeting.)

CHALLENGE/ACTION STEPS

1. What is one thing you learned about temptation because of this study?

2. Complete the sentence "For me, the most difficult area in dealing with temptation is . . . "

3. How can you apply the Top 10 Tips for Taking on Temptation to your situation?

4. What can we do as a small group to help keep you accountable?

Overview

You're Not Like Me!
(James 2:2-13)

TOPIC
Racism and prejudice

DESCRIPTION
The evils of racism and prejudice are alive and well today. Sadly enough, they are just as alive in the Church as they are in our world. This lesson tackles the issue head-on to see what God's Word has to say about it. Our desire is that students would be able to walk away with a new appreciation for others who are not like them, whether the difference is one of ethnicity, status, wealth or any other aspect.

KEY VERSE
"If you really keep the royal law found in the Scripture, 'Love your neighbor as yourself,' you are doing right. But if you show favoritism, you sin and are convicted by the law as lawbreakers." James 2:8-9

BIBLICAL BASIS
Genesis 1:26; Psalm 134:14; Matthew 7:1-6,24; John 7:24; James 2:2-13

THE BIG IDEA
In Jesus Christ, we are all one, regardless of race, wealth, status or any other difference.

SESSION AIMS
During this session you will guide students to do the following:
- Examine what the Bible has to say about the issue of prejudice
- Discover the ways in which we show prejudice today
- Implement a choice to live a lifestyle of equality, unity and love

PREPARATION
None

Outline

You're Not Like Me!
(James 2:2-13)

> **The Big Idea**
> In Jesus Christ, we are all one, regardless of race, wealth, status or any other difference.

INTRODUCTION

According to Webster's dictionary, "racism" is defined as "a belief that race is the primary determinant of human traits and capacities and that racial differences produce an inherent superiority of a particular race," and "prejudice" is defined as "preconceived judgment or opinion [or] an irrational attitude of hostility directed against an individual, a group, a race, or their supposed characteristics."[1]

> **Discussion**
> - How would you define "racism" and "prejudice"?
> - Where did you get your ideas about racism or prejudice?
> - What is the most damaging aspect of racism and prejudice?
> - How do racism and prejudice hurt everyone?

IN THE WORD

Racism and prejudice are not windows through which God wants us to view each other.

> **Discussion**
> - How do you think God feels about racism and prejudice?
> - Why do we often treat some people better than others?
> - How do we use appearance, ability, status or possessions to show prejudice or favoritism toward others?

I. Prejudice Is a Form of Judging—James 2:2-4

A. When we show favoritism or racism we are really judging others as better or worse than we are.

B. Read James 2:2. We are not to judge by appearance.

C. Read Matthew 7:1-6. God is hard-core when it comes to our judging others.

   1. "In the same way you judge others, you will be judged" (Matthew 7:2).

   2. Read Matthew 7:3-5. It is more important to look at our own faults than to judge others.

   3. Read John 7:24. There are times we must make judgments (e.g., in our choice of who to trust), but we need to base those kinds of judgments on God's Word and truth.

II. Prejudice Insults God's Creation—James 2:5-7

A. When we show prejudice, we insult God by belittling what He has created.

   1. Read Genesis 1:26. We are made in God's image.

   2. We are *all* "fearfully and wonderfully made" (Psalm 139:14).

B. When we show prejudice, we are saying that God must have made a mistake.

III. God Calls Us to Love Others Regardless of Our Differences—James 2:8-13

A. It can be hard to love others who are not like us.

   1. Often we attach conditions to our love of others.

   2. We think life would be better if others were more like us.

B. Read James 2:8. We are to love others as we love ourselves.

C. Read James 2:13. We are called to be merciful.

Discussion
- What conditions do we attach to others before we love them?
- What does it mean to "love others regardless of our differences"?
- What are some practical ways in which we can love others who are not like us?
- Why is it tough to show mercy to others?
- Why should we be merciful?
- How can we practically show mercy to others regardless of who they are?

CHALLENGE/ACTION STEPS

1. Is there someone you need to ask for forgiveness for showing them prejudice?
2. How has this study changed the way you look at others?
3. Think of what you can do this week to accomplish the following:
   - Stop judging
   - Celebrate the uniqueness of others as God's original creations
   - Show love regardless of differences
   - Be a person of mercy

Note
1. *Merriam-Webster's Collegiate Dictionary*, 10th ed., s.v. "racism" and "prejudice."

Overview

Don't Just Stand There—Do Something!
(James 2:14-26)

TOPIC
Faith versus works

DESCRIPTION
Are we saved by faith alone? Are we saved by what we do? These questions have caused dissension, confusion and division in the Church. This lesson will focus on the point that we are saved by faith, but true faith and transformation lead to a changed life—and to works that are the true fruit of that saving faith.

KEY VERSE
"As the body without the spirit is dead, so faith without deeds is dead." James 2:26

BIBLICAL BASIS
Luke 23:32-43; John 1:12; 3:16; Acts 16:31; 26:20; Romans 3:28; 10:9-10; Ephesians 2:8-10; Philippians 2:12-13; 1 Timothy 6:18; Hebrews 10:24-25; James 2:14-26; John 3:16-18

THE BIG IDEA
True faith means following Christ to the point of letting your faith change you *and* your actions.

SESSION AIMS
During this session you will guide students to do the following:
- Examine what God's Word has to say about the issue of faith versus works
- Discover what it means to have an alive faith in Christ
- Implement a choice to put their faith into action

PREPARATION
- Three pieces of poster board
- A felt-tip pen

Use the felt-tip pen to write "agree," disagree" and "clueless"—one word on each of the poster boards.

Outline

DON'T JUST STAND THERE—DO SOMETHING!

(JAMES 2:14-26)

> **The Big Idea**
> True faith means following Christ to the point of letting your faith change you *and* your actions.

INTRODUCTION

Begin by having the entire group stand. Hang the poster boards reading "agree," "disagree" and "clueless" in three different places in the room. After you read each statement below, give students the opportunity to vote whether they agree, disagree or don't know by moving to one of the signs in the room. If time allows, you may want to have a few students share their reasons for voting the way they did—encourage them to back up their positions with Scripture.

- We are saved by what we believe.
- We are saved by what we do.
- All we need to do to be saved is ask Jesus into our hearts.
- A person's walk with Jesus can be judged by the fruit in his or her life.
- You only believe as much as you live.

IN THE WORD

We can't earn our way into heaven. It's not a ticket we can buy. Faith in Christ is all that is required. So does this mean that as long as we believe in Jesus, we can live selfishly, ignoring the needs of others? Absolutely not—true faith changes our hearts and we begin to do good works because our hearts are called to serve others.

> **Suggestion**
> In this study outline, you'll be looking up different passages of Scripture dealing with the relationship between faith and works. Look up the passages first and ask, **What does this have to say about faith and works?** Allow for answers; then go over the specific points. Students should wrestle a little bit with the issue, so be ready to play devil's advocate with your group.

I. True Faith Leads to Salvation—Ephesians 2:8-10

There is nothing we can do to earn our salvation; it is only through faith that we are saved.

A. Read Luke 23:32-43. The only difference between the two criminals beside Jesus on the cross was that one mocked Him and one believed in Him.

B. Read John 1:12; 3:16. The key to heaven is simply believing that Christ died for our sins and accepting the grace of God through Jesus.

C. Read Acts 16:31. It's not enough to claim to believe; you have to truly accept Christ in your heart.

D. Read Romans 3:28; 10:9-10. Faith is more than being religious and following the rules.

E. Read Ephesians 2:8-10. Faith is accepting God's grace, which cannot be earned.

Discussion
- How is a person saved?
- Why do people need to be saved?
- Why is it difficult to share the message of Christ with others?

II. True Faith Leads to a Lifestyle Change—A Transformation

A. Read Acts 26:20. Faith in Christ will result in repentance and changing our ways.

B. Read Philippians 2:12-13. When we have faith, we allow God to work within to change us.

C. Read James 2:14-26. Seeing the needs of others is not enough; true faith will cause us to act upon what we see.

Discussion
- What is destructive about having faith without works or a changed lifestyle?
- How is being a Christian supposed to change the way we live?
- What are some areas in your life that you need God to help you change or work on?

III. True Faith Leads to Action

A. We obey, not to *be* saved, but because we *are* saved.

B. We are commanded to "do good, to be rich in good deeds, and to be generous and willing to share" (1 Timothy 6:18).

C. Read Hebrews 10:24-25. We should encourage one another, remembering what God has done for us.

D. Read 1 John 3:16-18. We are commanded to remember the sacrifice Christ made for us and to treat each other with the same love and compassion as Jesus shows.

Discussion
- What are some ways Christians can live out faith in their actions?
- How can living out our faith in action show the world who Jesus is?
- What action do you need to take in living out your faith?

CHALLENGE/ACTION STEPS

1. Do you have a true faith—a saving relationship with Jesus Christ?
2. What is the relationship between faith and works?
3. How can you show a greater faith in God this week?
4. What can we do as a group to put our faith in Christ into action to love and serve others while sharing His love?

Suggestion
Have students suggest some possible service or mission projects. Have them vote on which one to do. Within the next month or so, go as a group and serve together. Serving together will be an incredible bonding experience for the group.

Overview

STICKS AND STONES
(JAMES 3:3-8)

TOPIC
Taming our tongues

DESCRIPTION
Each one of us possesses the most powerful weapon in the world—words. "Sticks and stones may break my bones, but words will never hurt me!" is the old adage. Yet in our world, we know the truth; words do hurt us—and the emotional scars often last longer than physical pain does. Scripture calls us to weigh our words carefully, knowing that within them lies the power to build up or to destroy those around us. In this message, we'll be examining the power of our words and how we can use them to build others up.

KEY VERSE
"Out of the same mouth come praise and cursing. My brothers, this should not be." James 3:10

BIBLICAL BASIS
Proverbs 10:18-19,32; 11:12; Matthew 12:34-36; Acts 11:23; 15:37-39; Romans 14:1; Ephesians 4:29; Hebrews 10:24; James 3:3-8

THE BIG IDEA
The words you speak have the power to build up or tear down those around you.

SESSION AIMS
During this session you will guide students to do the following:
- Examine what God's Word has to say about the words that we speak
- Discover the power we have in the words that we use
- Implement a lifestyle built upon building others up with the words that we speak

PREPARATION

- A trash can
- A mirror
- A gift-wrapped box

Outline

STICKS AND STONES
(JAMES 3:3-8)

> **The Big Idea**
> The words you speak have the power to build up or tear down those around you.

INTRODUCTION

Hold up each item beginning with the trash can and ask: **How does this item represent the words that we speak?** Allow time to respond before going on to the next item. During responses, ask students to give examples or Scriptures that might help them explain their insight. Use the following points:

- Ephesians 4:29—Sometimes the words that we speak are useless (trash) in building others up.
- Matthew 12:34—Our words reflect (mirror) what's in our hearts.
- Hebrews 10:24—Our words can be encouragement (gifts) in the lives of others, treasures to be held.

IN THE WORD

Each one of us has been encouraged by what someone else has said, and each one of us has been hurt by the words of others. We are called to use the power of our words to build each other up, not tear each other down.

> **Discussion**
> - When was a time when you were built up by someone's words?
> - When was a time when you were destroyed by someone's words?
> - How can a person be hurt by what others say?
> - If every word you spoke in the past week was tape-recorded, what would you want to edit?

I. Encouragement Goes a Long Way—Romans 14:1

A. "A man who lacks judgment derides his neighbor, but a man of understanding holds his tongue" (Proverbs 11:12).

B. Read Acts 15:37-39. Sometimes encouraging others isn't the popular thing to do.

C. Read Acts 11:23. Encouragement goes a long way. When everyone else wanted to give up on Mark, Barnabas believed in Mark's sincerity and gave him another chance.

II. We Will Be Held Accountable—Matthew 12:34-36

We may think words aren't damaging, but God takes our every word seriously.

A. "Whoever spreads slander is a fool" (Proverbs 10:18).

B. "When words are many, sin is not absent, but he who holds his tongue is wise" (Proverbs 10:19).

C. "The lips of the righteous know what is fitting" (Proverbs 10:32).

Discussion

- What can you learn about a person by the words that he or she speaks?
- What is significant about the way we talk?
- How can we sin by the words that we speak?
- What do the word pictures in James 3:3-8 tell us about the words we speak?
- What is so difficult about taming the tongue?
- How can our tongues be used to build others up, rather than tear them down?

CHALLENGE/ACTION STEPS

1. We need to believe in others and encourage them. Believing in others means seeing their positives and their potential, rather than picking out their faults and weaknesses.

2. We need to build each other up. Take to heart the power your words can have on others. Make a decision to use your words to build others up.

3. We need to be active with our encouragement. Take action with your words and speak out! Make it a habit to build others up with your words.

4. We need to evaluate how well we encourage others. Ask yourself the following questions:

   - *What do I need to change or improve about the words that I speak?*
   - *Who is one person that I can encourage this week?*
   - *How can I be active with my encouragement this week?*

Overview

Got Wisdom?
(James 3:13-18)

TOPIC
Wisdom

DESCRIPTION
We live in a world that is at war with the things of God. What the world values and sees as wise is radically different than what God values as wise. Every day we make a choice—whether conscious or subconscious—to seek after worldly wisdom or godly wisdom. The outcome is seen in the actions and the depth of character of the person. This lesson takes a look at the two types of wisdom, their characteristics and their consequences.

KEY VERSE
"But the wisdom that comes from heaven is first of all pure; then peace-loving, considerate, submissive, full of mercy and good fruit, impartial and sincere." James 3:17

BIBLICAL BASIS
Psalm 19:7-11; Proverbs 3:13-18; 4:5-7; 9:10-12; 11:2; 12:8; 13:10; 17:24; 1 Corinthians 1:18-31; James 3:13-18; 1 John 2:15-17

THE BIG IDEA
Godly wisdom leads to life. Worldly wisdom leads to death.

SESSION AIMS
During this session you will guide students to do the following:
- Examine two different types of wisdom and values
- Discover the outcome of both types of wisdom
- Implement a choice to seek after and live by godly wisdom

PREPARATION
- Paper

- Pens or pencils
- A white board and dry-erase marker

Write the following Scripture references at the top of the white board: Proverbs 3:13-18; 4:5-7; 9:10-12; 11:2; 12:8; 13:10; 17:24.

Outline

Got Wisdom?

(James 3:13-18)

> **The Big Idea**
> Godly wisdom leads to life. Worldly wisdom leads to death.

INTRODUCTION

Distribute paper and pens or pencils and give the following instructions: **Without using words, draw a picture of how you would define the word "wisdom."** After drawing their pictures, have each student explain his or her drawing.

IN THE WORD

Wisdom is found in knowing God's heart and being humble enough to seek His will.

I. Godly Wisdom Does Not Boast—James 3:13-18

A. True wisdom is proven in our actions.
   1. Read James 3:14-16. Envy and selfish ambition are worldly.
   2. Godly wisdom is "pure; then peace-loving, considerate, submissive, full of mercy and good fruit, impartial and sincere" (James 3:17-18).
B. Read 1 Corinthians 1:18-31. True wisdom is proven in our words.
   1. Worldly wisdom boasts of intelligence.
   2. Godly wisdom boasts of the works of the Lord.
C. Read 1 John 2:15-17. Earthly desires and material possessions will pass away, but the wisdom of the Lord is eternal.

> **Discussion**
> Point to the list on the board and ask: **What do these verses say about wisdom and being wise?** Write responses on the board.

II. We Can Ask God for His Wisdom—James 1:5

A. Read Psalm 19:7-11. We can seek God's wisdom through His Word.

B. Read Proverbs 9:10. We can seek God's wisdom through a relationship with Him.

Discussion

- Which of the characteristics listed in James 3:17-18 impacts you the most?
- Which of them do you want to see developed in your life?
- Read Proverbs 9:10. What does it mean to "fear the Lord"? How does that lead to wisdom?

CHALLENGE/ACTION STEPS

1. Where do you seek wisdom?
2. What can you do this week to seek after God's wisdom, rather than worldly wisdom?

Overview

Looking Out for Number One
(James 4:1-12)

TOPIC
Pride versus humility

DESCRIPTION
One of the biggest battles we face in our lives is the battle between pride and humility. Students live in a world that tells them to look out for themselves and to forget others! James has told us to submit to God, seek humility and seek to be friends with God. All of these things are contrary to the world in which we live. In this study, you'll be looking at what it takes to look out for what is the true number one priority: the cause of Jesus Christ!

KEY VERSE
"You adulterous people, don't you know that friendship with the world is hatred toward God? Anyone who chooses to be a friend of the world becomes an enemy of God. God opposes the proud but gives grace to the humble." James 4:4,6

BIBLICAL BASIS
Genesis 1:27; Jeremiah 9:23-24; Matthew 20:26-27; John 13:2-27; 15:5; Romans 3:10; 1 Corinthians 1:26-31; Philippians 2:3-11; James 4:1-12

THE BIG IDEA
Pride leads to problems, but humility leads to greatness in the kingdom of God.

SESSION AIMS
During this session you will guide students to do the following:
- Examine what God's Word says is true humility
- Discover what things keep us from humility in our own lives
- Implement a choice to live a life of humility and servanthood

PREPARATION

- Trophies (various shapes and sizes and for various events)
- A $20 bill
- A toy car
- Cleaning supplies
- A basin filled with water
- A towel (an old one you don't want back)
- A pair of scissors

Outline

Looking Out for Number One
(James 4:1-12)

The Big Idea
Pride leads to problems, but humility leads to greatness in the kingdom of God.

INTRODUCTION
Relate how each of the following items might represent either humility or pride:
- Trophies—Things we hold onto to feel significant because of an achievement or accomplishment in some area. "Look at what I did (or can do)!"
- $20 bill—Seeking after money as a way to show status, greatness or pride.
- Toy car—Status symbol; pride in a possession.
- Cleaning supplies—Having someone serve you, or humility as a servant yourself.
- Basin of water and a towel—Jesus' example of true servanthood and selflessness.

IN THE WORD
Pride robs God of the glory, honor and praise that belongs to Him. God is the only One who deserves glory, honor and praise. He created us and is the source of all we do.

I. See the Truth of Your Pride—James 4:6

A. Pride leads to problems; humility leads to greatness in the kingdom of God.

B. Read James 4:1-12. Pride takes the credit for all we are and all we can do away from the One who gave it to us: God.
   1. Read Genesis 1:27. There is only one reason we exist to do any of the great things we do: God called us into existence.
   2. We were created for God's purposes, not our own.
   3. We can do nothing apart from God (see John 15:5).
   4. The world says that we are basically good. Romans 3:10 reminds us that no one is good—righteous.

> **Discussion**
> - How would you define the word "humility"?
> - What does the world think about humility?
> - Read Philippians 2:3-11. What do you think it means in verse 7 that Jesus "made himself nothing"?
> - How is this completely different from what the world tells us to do?

II. Put God Back on the Throne—Philippians 2:3

A. We can be so busy with ourselves that even God gets our leftover attention. Humility means stopping our obsession with our own agenda and allowing God to take His rightful place of number one in our lives.

B. Read Jeremiah 9:23-24. Don't boast of your achievements, possessions or giftedness; boast that you know God.

   1. See yourself for who you are—and realize that you are nothing without God.
   2. See God for who He is and what He's done.
   3. Boasting in the Lord is giving Him the glory for the things we want to take credit for.
   4. Boasting in the Lord means boasting in what He has done for your salvation (see 1 Corinthians 1:26-31).

> **Discussion**
> - What are some of the consequences of only thinking about yourself?
> - How have you seen those consequences lived out in those around you?
> - What would be some of the benefits of focusing on others?
> - What is one thing in which you can boast about God?
> - Why is God jealous for His glory? What difference does it make?
> - Is there an area of your life in which you've been a glory hog—taking credit for the glory that really belongs to God?

III. Express Humility Through Servanthood—John 13:2-27

A. Jesus gave us the greatest example of humility, by washing the disciples' feet. Servanthood and humility are linked together; you cannot experience true humility if you are not willing to be a servant.

B. Read Matthew 20:26-27. God places a high calling on serving one another.

Discussion
- Why is it so difficult to have a servant's heart?
- How do servanthood and humility go together?
- What keeps you from being more of a servant?
- What will you do about it this week?

CHALLENGE/ACTION STEPS

This week, set the P-A-C-E.

P—Are you *prideful* or humble? Where is your heart?

A—*Admit* (confess) any pride in your life.

C—*Choose* to give God the glory.

E—*Express* your servanthood. Find one thing you can do this week to serve someone else.

Suggestion

Take the towel from the introductory illustration and have students cut off a piece of it to take with them as a visual reminder of being a person of humility.

Overview

I'm So Confused!

(James 4:13-17)

TOPIC
God's will for our lives

DESCRIPTION
Young people are making some of the most important decisions of their lives. Our role is to help them make wise and right choices in life. In this study, we'll be looking at the decisions we face and how to make wise ones.

KEY VERSE
"Instead, you ought to say, 'If it is the Lord's will, we will live and do this or that.'"
James 4:15

BIBLICAL BASIS
2 Chronicles 19:6; Psalm 119:11,105; Proverbs 3:5-6; 8:10-11,17; 13:1,20; 15:12,22; 20:25; Galatians 6:7-8; Ephesians 5:15,17; Philippians 4:6-7; James 3:13-18; 4:15

THE BIG IDEA
God needs to be at the very center of our decision making.

SESSION AIMS
During this session you will guide students to do the following:
- Examine what God's Word has to say about decision making
- Discover biblical principles for making wise decisions
- Implement a lifestyle of seeking God's will in all decision making

PREPARATION
- Paper
- Pens or pencils
- A white board and dry-erase marker

Write the following Scripture references at the top of the white board: Matthew 6:33-34; Philippians 4:6; 2 Timothy 3:16-17; Romans 12:2; James 1:5-8; 3:13-18; 4:13-17; Proverbs 11:14; 18:13; 20:5,18.

Outline

I'm So Confused!

(James 4:13-17)

The Big Idea
God needs to be at the very center of our decision making.

INTRODUCTION

Have students form groups of two or three. Distribute paper and pens or pencils and instruct each group to come up with a realistic four- or five-sentence situation or problem that needs to be solved. It can be about a relationship, a question of ethics or a situation that involves compromise and needs to end with "So what would you do?" Allow a few minutes for groups to brainstorm; then have them exchange case studies with another group and come up with a solution to the problem they now have. If time allows (and you have more than two groups), have groups exchange case studies again to give another group a chance to solve the problem.

IN THE WORD

When we face tough choices, there are three principles we can apply to help us make our final decisions.

Discussion
Point to the list on the white board and ask: **What decision-making principles can be found in God's Word?** Write responses on the board.

I. Know the Consequences—Galatians 6:7-8

A. We reap what we sow.

B. The consequences of our decisions aren't always seen right away.

  1. "The one who sows to please his sinful nature, from that nature will reap destruction; the one who sows to please the Spirit, from the Spirit will reap eternal life" (Galatians 6:8).

2. Read Proverbs 8:10-11. We need to make sound choices based on more than what's readily apparent; we need to think about what's really valuable in the long term.

3. "It is a trap for a man to dedicate something rashly and only later to consider his vows" (Proverbs 20:25).

II. Seek a God View—Proverbs 3:5

A. "Consider carefully what you do, because you are not judging for man but for the LORD, who is with you whenever you give a verdict" (2 Chronicles 19:6).

B. "Be very careful, then, how you live . . . understand what the Lord's will is" (Ephesians 5:15,17).

1. Read Psalm 119:11,105. We should spend time with God reading His Word.

2. Read Philippians 4:6-7. We should spend time praying to God and seeking His voice.

3. Read Proverbs 3:5-6. We should spend time getting to know who God is.

III. Get an Outside View—Proverbs 8:17

A. Read Proverbs 13:1; 15:12. Only a fool believes he or she has all the answers.

B. Read Proverbs 13:20. We are influenced by those we spend time with.

C. Read Proverbs 15:22. Our best avenue for making good decisions is to seek the advice of others.

1. We should seek advice from those who will be truthful.

2. Read James 3:13. We should seek advice from those who set a godly example in both their words and their lives.

3. We should seek advice from more than one source.

4. We shouldn't make quick decisions; we should pray about them first.

CHALLENGE/ACTION STEPS

1. Think about a recent tough decision you faced. Which of the three principles you have just learned would have been the most helpful in making your decision and why?

2. If you've already made your decision, how do you think the principles you just learned would have impacted the outcome; what would you do differently based on what you learned in this lesson?

3. If you've not yet made the decision, how can you apply the principles you just learned to help in your choice?

Suggestion

Encourage students to apply these biblical decision-making principles to an upcoming decision this week. At the beginning of the next meeting, have them share the experience and outcome.

Overview

ME, MYSELF AND MINE!
(JAMES 5:1-6)

TOPIC
Materialism

DESCRIPTION
We live a world dominated by materialism. We judge others' worth and our own worth by the possessions we have. God's Word has a lot to say about materialism—its impact and its cure. This lesson will explore the effects of materialism, helping students see the destructive power of personal greed and the blessing of stewardship and giving.

KEY VERSE
"Your gold and silver are corroded. Their corrosion will testify against you and eat your flesh like fire. You have hoarded wealth in the last days." James 5:3

BIBLICAL BASIS
1 Chronicles 29:3; Matthew 6:19-21,24; 19:21; Luke 12:15-21; 2 Corinthians 9:6-8,10-13; Philippians 4:19; 1 Timothy 6:6-10,17; Hebrews 11:26; James 5:1-6

THE BIG IDEA
God's cure for the disease of materialism is found in giving.

SESSION AIMS
During this session you will guide students to do the following:
* Examine what God's Word has to say about materialism
* Discover their own personal responsibility with their possessions
* Implement an attitude of other-centeredness and open-handedness

PREPARATION
* Paper
* Pens or pencils

Outline

ME, MYSELF AND MINE!
(JAMES 5:1-6)

> **The Big Idea**
> God's cure for the disease of materialism is found in giving.

INTRODUCTION

Distribute paper and pens or pencils. Instruct students to create a list of all the things they are wearing, including anything in their pockets. Next to each item have them write down an estimate of how much each item costs. Have volunteers share their totals. Explain: **All of us have so much. Maybe even more than we may think at times. We live in a materialistic society—one that focuses so much on what we have.**

> **Discussion**
> * If your house were on fire (and everyone was safe) and you could only save three things, what would they be? Why?
> * What does Matthew 6:21 tell you about where your heart is?

IN THE WORD

The world in which we live has a different view than God of what is valuable. The world tells us that contentment and happiness can be found in earthly things, all of which are temporary. God tells us that true contentment and happiness are only found when we look for things eternal—such as a relationship with Him.

> **Discussion**
> * Read Matthew 6:19-21,24; James 5:1-6. What messages does the world give us when it comes to possessions?
> * What choice do we need to make and why is it so difficult to make it?
> * Read 1 Timothy 6:6-10. How does the world define "contentment" and "happiness"?
> * What are the consequences of loving money; what are some of the problems people encounter because of it?
> * Is it possible for a Christian to be rich and still be obedient and love God?

I. Learn to Trust in God, Not in Wealth—1 Timothy 6:17

A. God calls us to put our trust in Him, not in wealth.
1. We are called to put our "hope in God" (1 Timothy 6:17), not in material things.
2. Read Philippians 4:19. God will meet our needs, not necessarily our wants.

B. Read Luke 12:15-21. Wealth is temporal; God is eternal.

C. Read 1 Chronicles 29:3. King David was a powerful, rich ruler, yet he gave his personal treasures to honor God because he treasured God above all else.
1. "A man's life does not consist in the abundance of his possessions" (Luke 12:15).
2. Read Matthew 6:19. Earthly treasures are temporary and will eventually wither away.

II. Learn to Give

A. Read Matthew 19:21. If called upon, we must be willing to give up everything to follow Christ.
1. God will provide everything we need when we focus on Him. Read Hebrews 11:26. Moses gave up his inheritance as the adopted son of Pharaoh's daughter because he valued more his inheritance in the kingdom of heaven.
2. Read 2 Corinthians 9:6-8. What we give, we will receive.

B. "For where your treasure is, there your heart will be also" (Matthew 6:21).

Discussion
- Why is it sometimes hard to give with a cheerful attitude?
- According to 2 Corinthians 9:8, what are we promised by God?
- How does giving loosen the grip of materialism in our lives?

CHALLENGE/ACTION STEPS

1. What does 2 Corinthians 9:10-13 remind us about our wealth? What does it mean in practical terms for each of us?
2. What do you need to do this week to trust more in God than in your wealth?
3. What can you do this week to give in response to what God has done for you?
4. What is one way in which you will be different because of what you learned in this lesson?

Overview

HELLO, GOD! ARE YOU THERE?
(JAMES 5:13-20)

TOPIC
Prayer

DESCRIPTION
Prayer is one of the most powerful tools we have to come to know our heavenly Father in a more intimate way, yet how often do our prayer lives develop into a grocery list for God? Prayer is much more than a time to list our requests. Prayer is our lifeline to the Father, a way for us to commune with Him. In this lesson the role and impact of prayer in our lives as believers will be explored.

KEY VERSE
"The prayer of a righteous man is powerful and effective." James 5:16

BIBLICAL BASIS
Psalms 23; 38:18; 86:5; 102:11-12; 150:6; Proverbs 28:13; Matthew 7:7; 1 Thessalonians 5:18; James 5:13-20; 1 John 5:14-15

THE BIG IDEA
Prayer is communion with God.

SESSION AIMS
During this session you will guide students to do the following:
- Examine the role and impact of prayer in the life of the believer
- Discover the elements of an effective prayer life
- Implement a commitment to pray on a regular basis

PREPARATION
- Paper
- Pens or pencils
- A white board and a dry-erase marker

Write the following questions on the white board:
1. What words come to mind when you think of the word "prayer"?
2. What issues do you find it easy to pray about?
3. What issues do you find it difficult to pray about?
4. What is the biggest barrier you have in praying?

Outline

HELLO, GOD! ARE YOU THERE?

(JAMES 5:13-20)

The Big Idea
Prayer is communion with God.

INTRODUCTION

Distribute paper and pens or pencils and instruct students to write their answers to the questions on the white board—without discussing them aloud. Allow a few minutes for writing; then ask volunteers to share their answers. Be sure to ask why they answered each question the way they did.

IN THE WORD

Prayer is a vital ingredient in developing intimacy with God. It's not fancy words or rhyming chants; prayer is about communion with God. Too many times we treat prayer like a vending machine. Prayer is so much more than just asking God for the things we need—or think we need.

I. We Pray to Praise—Psalm 150:6

A. "Let everything that has breath praise the LORD" (Psalm 150:6).
  1. Even when we don't want anything from God, we should pray and thank Him for all He has provided for us.
  2. Read Psalm 102:11-12. Although the psalmist was suffering, he continually praised God's goodness and character.
  3. Read James 5:13-20. We are called to pray in good times and bad.

Discussion
- Why is it important to have a consistent attitude of praise to God for who He is?
- How can adoring God positively impact your life?
- If God were physically sitting beside you, what would you want to say to Him about who He is?

II. We Pray to Admit Sin—Psalm 86:5

A. After we praise God and all He has done for us, we realize how much we have fallen short of His will, how much we have sinned against Him.

   1. Read Psalm 38:18. We are not worthy of God's love or forgiveness.

   2. Read Proverbs 28:13. When we confess our sins, we find mercy.

B. God knows our hearts and wants us to admit our failure and be repentant.

Discussion
- Why is it difficult to admit our sin to God?
- What are God's promises in these verses?
- What do we need to do to unlock those promises?

III. We Pray to Acknowledge—1 Thessalonians 5:18

A. After we have confessed our sin, we are free to thank God for all that He has done for us, especially His forgiveness.

B. Developing an attitude of thankfulness is life altering and soul renewing.

C. Thankfulness reminds us of our desperate need for God.

D. Thankfulness humbly places us in our rightful position and God in His.

Discussion
- How do you think God feels when we thank Him? When we complain?
- What does it mean to be thankful in all situations?
- What are five things you can give thanks for today?

IV. We Pray to Ask—Matthew 7:7

A. After we have given God His rightful place and we are in our rightful place, then we can come to God with our requests.

B. God cares about what's going on in our lives and knows everything that happens to us.

   1. God wants us to include Him in what's going on.

   2. Prayer is a conversation with God, talking to Him about our fears, dreams, desires and needs.

C. Read 1 John 5:14-15. When we are in God's will, our requests will be honored.

CHALLENGE/ACTION STEPS

1. What is your greatest need right now?

2. What keeps you from experiencing prayer on a deeper level? What will you do about it this week?

3. Perhaps one of the greatest prayers in all of Scripture is found in Psalm 23. Spend a few minutes reading through that psalm together. Give each student a piece of paper and a pencil. Have them rewrite Psalm 23 in their own words. After everyone is finished writing, have a few volunteers read their own version of Psalm 23.

4. Spend the last five minutes in silent prayer with the group. As the leader, guide your students through this time by giving them approximately one minute per element of prayer—adoration, admitting, acknowledging and asking.

> **Suggestion**
> Check with students during the week to see how everyone is doing on his or her commitment to experience prayer on a deeper level.

SCRIPTURE REFERENCE INDEX

OLD TESTAMENT

Bold numbers indicate Key Verses.

Bold numbers indicate Key Verses.

NEW TESTAMENT

Bold numbers indicate Key Verses.

Bold numbers indicate Key Verses.

Bold numbers indicate Key Verses.

More Great Ways to Reach and Teach Young People

So You Want to Be a Wise Guy
An outrageous group study for junior high
Manual
ISBN 08307.29178

Dave's Complete Guide to Junior High Ministry
An all-in-one, practical, hands-on guide for everything relating to junior high ministry
Dave Veerman
Paperback
ISBN 08307.27604

GP4U (God's Plan for You)
A middle school/junior high group study
Kara Eckmann Powell
Reproducible
ISBN 08307.24060

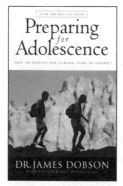

Preparing for Adolescence
Dr. James Dobson
Paperback
ISBN 08307.24974

Guide to Childhood Development
Mass
ISBN 08307.24990

Family Guide and Workbook
Manual
ISBN 08307.25016

Growth Guide Manual
ISBN 08307.25024

Group Guide
ISBN 08307.25008

Family Tape Pack—8 Audiocassettes
ISBN 08307.26357

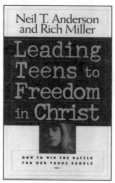

Leading Teens to Freedom in Christ
How to win the battle for our young people
Neil T. Anderson
and *Rich Miller*
Paperback
ISBN 08307.18400

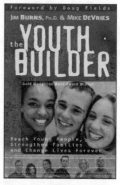

The YouthBuilder
Reaching young people for Christ and changing lives forever
Jim Burns
and *Mike DeVries*
Paperback
ISBN 08307.29232

Gospel Light

Available at your local Christian bookstore
www.gospellight.com

Pulse — GOD'S WORD FOR A JR. HIGH WORLD

"This is the best junior high/middle school curriculum to come out in years. Creativity and Biblical integrity are evident on every page. Students will love it."
—Jim Burns, Ph.D.
President
National Institute of Youth Ministry

Young people between the ages of 11 and 14 are the most open to who Jesus is and what a life with Him offers. Reach them with Pulse—designed especially for them!

Throughout the cutting-edge series, three categories of study help junior highers understand and apply God's Word in their lives: Biblical, Life Issues and Discipleship.

Connect with junior highers—get all the Pulse studies!

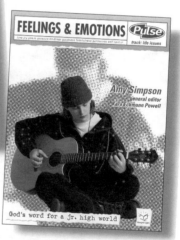

#1 Christianity: the Basics
ISBN 08307.24079

#2 Prayer
ISBN 08307.24087

#3 Friends
ISBN 08307.24192

#4 Teachings of Jesus
ISBN 08307.24095

#5 Followers of Christ
ISBN 08307.24117

#6 Teens of the Bible
ISBN 08307. 24125

#7 Life at School
ISBN 08307.25083

#8 Miracles of Jesus
ISBN 08307.25091

#9 Home and Family
ISBN 08307.25105

#10 Genesis
ISBN 08307.25113

#11 Fruit of the Spirit
ISBN 08307.25474

#12 Feelings & Emotions
ISBN 08307.25482

#13 Peer Pressure
ISBN 08307.25490

#14 Reaching Your World
ISBN 08307.25504

Available at your local Christian bookstore.
www.gospellight.com

041633

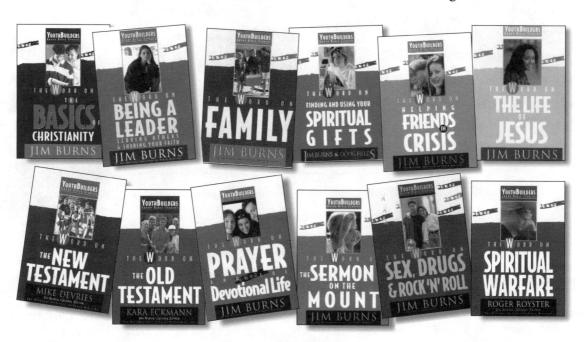

Wake 'Em Up!

This fresh-roasted blend of sizzling hot resources helps you turn youth meetings into dynamic events that kids look forward to. Successfully field-tested in youth groups and edited by youth expert **Jim Burns, Fresh Ideas** will wake 'em up and get your group talking.

Bible Study Outlines and Messages
ISBN 08307.18850

Case Studies, Talk Sheets and Starters
ISBN 08307.18842

Games, Crowdbreakers & Community Builders
ISBN 08307.18818

Illustrations, Stories and Quotes to Hang Your Message On
ISBN 08307.18834

Incredible Retreats
ISBN 08307.24036

Missions and Service Projects
ISBN 08307.18796

Skits and Dramas
ISBN 08307.18826

Worship Experiences
ISBN 08307.24044

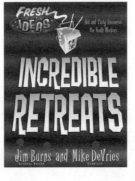

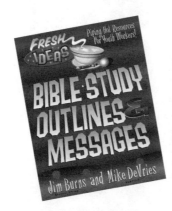

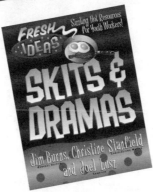

Gospel Light